Pressure Cooking
the Easy Way

Pressure Cooking the Easy Way

Healthy One-Pot Meals
Everyone Will Love

Maureen B. Keane
Daniella Chace

PRIMA PUBLISHING

PRIMA PUBLISHING and colophon are registered trademarks of Prima Communications, Inc.

Previously published under the title *The Ultimate Pressure Cooker Cookbook* by Prima Publishing, 1995.

Library of Congress Cataloging-in-Publication Data

Keane, Maureen.
      Pressure cooking the easy way : healthy one-pot meals everyone will love / Maureen B. Keane and Daniella Chace.
           p.   cm.
      Includes index.
      ISBN 0-7615-1285-3

      1. Pressure cookery.   I. Chace, Daniella.   II. Title.
TX840.P7K38   1997
641.5'87—dc21   97-40598
                                                                                    CIP

            01 HH 10 9 8 7

Printed in the United States of America

How to Order
Single copies may be ordered from Prima Publishing, 3000 Lava Ridge Court, Roseville, CA 95661; telephone (800) 632-8676. Quantity discounts are also available. On your letterhead, include information concerning the intended use of the books and the number of books you wish to purchase.

Visit us online at www.primalifestyles.com

To our agent, Sid Harriet, for all his help and support.

CONTENTS

Acknowledgments   xv

PART I: Your Pressure Cooker   1

CHAPTER 1

Getting Acquainted   3

The Parts of Your Pressure Cooker   4
Maintaining Your Pressure Cooker   6

CHAPTER 2

Basic Pressure Cooking   7

Advantages of Pressure Cooking   8
   Pressure Steaming   10
   Browning   10
   Pressure Cooking   11
   Releasing Pressure   11
Helpful Hints   12
Do's and Don'ts   13

CHAPTER 3

Common Questions and Answers   15

The Basics   15
Common Problems   17
Troubleshooting   18
Maintenance   19

PART II: The Recipes 21

CHAPTER 4

Red Meat 23

Tips for Cooking Meat 23
Nutrition Tips 24
Pork Chops with Apples and Roots 27
Beef and Vegetable Casserole 28
Variations
Tomato Pot Roast 28
Sweet Potato Pot Roast 29
Chili Pot Roast with Beans 29
Pineapple Pork with Honey Date Yams and Pearl
Onion Peas 30
Pot Roast with Onions and Root Vegetables 31
Beaujolais Lamb 32
Beef and Black Beans 33
Barbecue Steak with Maple Sweet Potatoes 34
Hearty Beef and Barley Casserole 35

CHAPTER 5

Poultry 37

Tips for Cooking Poultry 37
Nutrition Tips 38
Poached Chicken 40
Poultry Sauces
Confetti Sauce 40
Warm Curry Sauce 41
Sour Cream and Dill Sauce 41
Sherry Chicken with Garlic 42
Two Can Turkey 43
Variations
Mexican-Style Turkey 43
Italian Turkey Legs 43

Poultry Casserole   44
  Variations
  Ginger Chicken   44
  Creamed Turkey Casserole   45
Coconut Curry Chicken   46
Hawaiian Chicken   47
Chicken and Dumpling Casserole 48
Tomato Turkey Breast with Rosemary and
      Oregano   49
Champagne Chicken with Shallot Sauce and
      Apple Rice   50
Hot Nutty Game Hens   51

CHAPTER 6

Seafood   53

Tips for Cooking Seafood   53
Nutrition Tips   54
Tips for Buying Seafood   54
  Poached Fish with Julienned Vegetables   56
    Seafood Sauces
    Chipotle Cocktail Sauce   56
    Lemon-Tarragon Vinaigrette   57
    Basic Sauces
    Yogurt Sauces   57
    Mayonnaise Sauces   57
    Vegetable Sauces   58
    Fruit Sauces   58
    Vinaigrette Sauces   58
  Shrimp in Spicy Marinade   59
  Lobster Steamed in Beer   60
  Steamed Clams   61
  Orange Roughy with Mango   62
  Whole Fish in Red Curry Sauce with
      Lime Leaves   63
  Fish and Eggplant Curry   64

CHAPTER 7

Soups   65

Tips for Cooking Soup   65
Nutrition Tips   66
Stock   67
  Beef Stock   68
  Chicken Stock   68
  Vegetable Broth   69
  Almost Instant Soup   70
    Variations
    Chicken Garlic Soup with Greens   70
    Beef Noodle Soup   71
    Chunky Chicken Soup   71
    Ham and Bean Soup   71
  European Pea Soup   72
  Beef Borscht with Sour Cream and Dill   73
  Chicken Soup   74
  New England Clam Chowder   75
  Seafood and Saffron Soup   76
  Hearty Multibean Soup   77
  Minestrone   78
  Onion Soup   79
  Beer and Bacon Bean Soup   80
  White Bean Soup   81
  French Navy Bean Soup   82
  Cannellini Beans and Swiss Chard Soup   83

CHAPTER 8

Stews   85

Tips for Cooking Stews   85
Nutrition Tips   86
  Lamb Stew   87
  Quick Beef Stew   88

Variations
Beef and Bean Stew   88
Chicken Stew   89
Turkey-Vegetable Stew   89
Chicken and Chick-pea Stew   90
Spicy Vegetable Bean Stew   91
Moroccan Bean and Rice Stew   92
Cioppino   93
Savory Lentil Stew   94
Potato, Lentil, and Wild Mushroom Stew   95
Saffron Seafood Stew   96

CHAPTER 9

Vegetables   97

Tips for Cooking Vegetables   98
Nutrition Tips   98
Artichokes in Garlic Sauce   103
Vegetable Casserole   104
Variations
Frozen Vegie Casserole   105
Pesto Zucchini and Pepper   105
Sauces for Vegetables
Salmon Sauce   106
Hot Crab Sauce   106
Creamy Dill Sauce   106
Hot Curry Sauce   107
Cheese Sauce   107
Asparagus with Lemon-Dill Sauce   108
Glazed Carrots and Shallots   109
Ginger-Tomato Spaghetti Sauce   110
Mashed Sweet Potatoes with Balsamic
      Vinegar   111
Green Beans with Tomatoes and
      Sesame Seeds   112
Hot Potato Salad   113
Confetti Corn   114

CHAPTER 10

Fruit   115

Tips for Cooking Fresh Fruit   115
Tips for Cooking Dried Fruit   116
  Date-stuffed Apples   119
  Poached Company Fruit   120
    Variations
    Juice-poached Pears   120
    Poached Apples   121
  Stewed Dried Fruit   121
  Mixed Fruit Compote   122
    Variations
    Spicy Ginger Compote   122
    Raisin Topping   123
  Baked Oranges   124
  Brown Sugar Bananas   125

CHAPTER 11

Legumes   127

Tips for Cooking Legumes   128
Nutrition Tips   129
  Refried Black Beans   131
  Bean Casserole   132
    Variations
    Tomatoes and Beans   132
    Beans and Greens   132
    Spicy Beans   132
  Mediterranean Black Beans   133
  Refried Beans   134
  Lentil Hummus   135
  Spicy Vegetable Dahl   136
  Ham and Bean Hash   137
  Chick-peas and Chicken   138
  Mild Vegetarian Chili   139
  Bean and Chicken Enchiladas   140

CHAPTER 12

Grains 143

Tips for Cooking Grains   143
Nutrition Tips   144
  Rice Pilaf   146
    Variations
    Quick and Easy White Rice Pilaf   146
    Nutty Wild Rice Pilaf   147
    Mushroom Pilaf   147
  Steamed Rice   148
    Variations
    Steamed Seasoned White Rice   148
    Steamed Rice with Vegetables   149
    Steamed Rice with Fruit   149
  Savory Bulgur   150
  Bulgur Pilaf   151
  Green Pepper and Millet with Mushrooms   152
  Vegetable Risotto   153
  Barley Rice   154
  Millet Pilaf   155
  Savory Quinoa and Tomatoes   156
  Breakfast Molasses Wheat Flakes   157
  Vanilla Wheat Flakes with Golden Raisins   158
  Spicy Polenta   159
  Coconut Rice and Shrimp   160

CHAPTER 13

Custards, Puddings, and Steamed Breads   161

Tips for Cooking Custards, Puddings, and
  Steamed Breads   161
Nutrition Tips   162
  Tapioca Pudding   163
  Lemon Pudding   164

Variations
Orange Pudding   164
Coconut Pudding   165
Strawberry Pudding   165
Basic Egg Custard   166
Variations
Rich Egg Custard   166
Skinny Custard   167
Chocolate Custard   167
Caramel Custard   167
Bread and Butter Pudding   168
Variations
Lowfat Bread Pudding   169
Almond Prune Bread Pudding   169
Dated Bread Pudding with Caramel Sauce   169
Onion Bread Pudding   169
Boston Brown Bread   170

CHAPTER 14

Meals for One   171

Tips for Cooking for One   172
Nutrition Tips   172
Barbecue Steak with Yams and Honeyed
Banana   173
Stuffed Vegie Dinner with Baby Vegetables and
Poached Fruit   174
Variations
Stuffed Onion Dinner   175
Stuffed Zucchini Dinner   175
Lamb Chops with Creamy Dill Sauce, Jam, and
Bread Pudding   176
Aunt Maureen's Chicken Soup   178

Index   179

ACKNOWLEDGMENTS

We would like to thank the following individuals who provided pressure cookers and literature for our research: Fraser Laurie, Bo/Nash; Lydia Hawryluk and Virginia Kiremidjian, Farberware; Patricio Barriga, Fagor America; Jack Knipple, Hawkins Futura; Phil Ryan, Innovations; Joann O'Gara, National Presto Industries Inc.; Lonnie and Peter Bumann, Susamat; Rosey Pulaski, Wearever-Mirro; Philip Jacobs, Wisconsin Aluminum Foundry Company.

Thanks to our helpers and taste testers: John Keane, Tara Hubbard, Nels Moulton, Eric Moulton, Thad Nicolai, Merrilee Gomez, Nuria Gomez, Chauncey P. Dewey III, and our very special taster Buddy Dewey.

PART I

Your Pressure Cooker

Your grandmother had a secret. She knew how to prepare hearty stews, full-flavored soups, and fork-tender pot roasts with greater economy and more flavor and vitamins than her grandchildren. And she did it all without the aid of that newfangled invention, the microwave. Her secret was the pressure cooker. Today a whole new generation of cooks is discovering the many advantages of pressure cooking.

This once indispensable kitchen appliance is again in fashion as Americans try to eat more nutritiously in less time. For today's fast-paced lifestyle the pressure cooker can be the answer to every cook's prayer. It can turn out delicious meals in just a fraction of the time of conventional methods. The pressure cooker can be even faster than the microwave!

This book will teach you (or remind you) how to use the pressure cooker. Many recipes also give suggestions on how to vary ingredients to make your own special versions. Chapter 1 tells you how to use and care for your pressure cooker. Chapter 2 is a primer on how the pressure cooker works. Chapter 3 is for troubleshooting, and will answer frequently asked questions about getting along with your pressure cooker.

CHAPTER 1

Getting Acquainted

The pressure cooker comes in a wide variety of styles and models but the basic principles behind each one are the same. The outside of the cooker is usually aluminum. The inside is sometimes coated with a nonstick surface. A trivet or steamer basket is always included for steaming foods. A pressure regulator, often a weight that fits over the vent pipe, is built into the lid. A lift pin or pressure pop-up valve allows air in the cooker to escape and seals off to prevent steam from escaping. A sealing ring fits around the inner edge of the lid to form a tight pressure seal between the lid and the pot. An overpressure plug will pop off to release steam if the pressure rises too high.

To use your cooker properly, get to know the parts that make up your new machine. Read your instruction manual so you understand the features and limitations of your particular cooker. Pressure cookers come in a variety of sizes with a number of different lid shapes. One of the first decisions you make about buying a cooker is what size you need.

The smallest pressure cooker holds 4 quarts if filled to the brim. Since pressure cookers should never be filled more than

half or two-thirds full, the 4-quart models really only hold 2
quarts. The 6- to 8-quart model is a good size for most needs. A
larger cooker allows you to cook taller pieces of meat and more
courses at once.

If you plan on using your cooker to steam grains, you will
need one large enough to hold a rice bowl. The amount of water
you will need to maintain pressure varies according to the model
and size you buy, so be sure you read your instruction manual.

Most of your favorite recipes that involve steaming, brais-
ing, boiling, or stewing can be modified to take advantage of the
pressure cooker. Using the recipe instructions here as a general
guide, reduce the old cooking time by two-thirds.

Always add the minimum amount of liquid your cooker instructions recommend to allow the necessary steam to build up.
If the recipe calls for milk or a milk product, add it after you remove the cover at the end of cooking. Likewise, do not thicken
the dish until cooking is complete. If the recipe calls for a thick
ingredient such as tomato paste, dilute it with water before cooking then cook with the cover off to reduce.

The pressure cooker does not work well with recipes that
require dry heat, such as recipes that call for baking or roasting.

The Parts of Your Pressure Cooker

The pressure cooker is basically a pot or saucepan with a cover
that seals to the body of the pan. (See Figure 1.) Under the lid,
around the rim is the *gasket* or *sealing ring*. The gasket forms a tight
seal between the cover and the body of the cooker when the
cooker is closed. It is easily removed for cleaning.

The *pressure regulator* or *weight* is found on the cover. It sits on
top of the *vent pipe* and controls the buildup of pressure inside the
cooker. Some models have a single pressure weight which regulates pressure to 15 pounds per square inch (or psi), sometimes
called *high pressure*. Others have variable weights or a pressure regulator built into the handle of the cover. Your instruction booklet
will explain how your cooker regulates pressure.

The *lift pin*, or *pressure pop-up valve*, allows air to escape the closed cooker. As pressure builds up, the valve pops up, sealing the cover. If the vent pipe becomes clogged during cooking, the pop-up valve will release excess pressure. When the cooker is removed from its heat source and the pressure begins to drop, the valve falls. The cover of your pressure cooker should never be removed when the valve is up and locked. Dangerous burns can result. How level the burner is can also affect performance; a tilted burner can interfere with the regulator's work.

All pressure cookers also have an *overpressure plug* in the cover. This plug will blow out and allow excess steam to escape if the vent pipe becomes plugged. Once the overpressure plug has been released, it cannot be replaced. Read your instruction manual to find out how to order a replacement. Some models also have a *safety release lock* that prevents the cover from being removed until the pressure is released.

A *trivet* or *steamer basket* is included with most pressure cookers. This fits inside the cooker and is used to steam foods. The recipes in this book will tell you when to use the trivet. Visit your

Figure 1.   A standard pressure cooker.

local housewares store to shop for accessories for your cooker. Metal steamer baskets, higher trivets, and ovenproof casserole dishes that fit inside the cooker will all help to make your machine more versatile.

Maintaining Your Pressure Cooker

Pressure cookers are easy to maintain and clean. Most are made of aluminum and resist staining. Before you use your cooker for the first time, wash it in hot soapy water. Remove the gasket from around the underside of the cover and wash it as well. Be sure to rinse and dry thoroughly. Washing your cooker after each use as soon as possible will make food particles easier to remove. Stubborn stains require a steel wool pad or nonabrasive cleaner, and discolorations respond well to 2 teaspoons baking soda dissolved in 1 quart of water and boiled in the cooker or boiling equal amounts of vinegar and water. Always store your cooker with the lid upside down or off to prevent the buildup of odors in the pan.

After using your cooker, inspect the vent tube and lift pin for blockages. Hold the lid before a light and check to see if the tubes are open. If no light can be seen, use a piece of wire to open the vent then rinse with hot water.

These are just general instructions. Refer to your owners manual before you begin to use your cooker. If your pressure cooker is maintained properly, it will give you years of service and enjoyment.

CHAPTER 2

Basic Pressure Cooking

Pressure cookers have been around since the turn of the century in one form or another. Although today's cooker is much safer and easier to use, the principles behind pressure cooking have not changed.

Pressure cookers cook faster than other methods of cooking for the simple reason that the temperature inside of their pans is hotter than the temperature inside an open pan. When water is heated in an open pan, the water molecules absorb the heat applied to the bottom by the heating element. This energizes the water molecules and eventually they absorb enough energy to fly out of the pan and into the air as steam. The temperature at which this occurs is called the boiling point.

Boiling points differ depending on where you live because the amount of energy needed to push through the air molecules differs. The higher above sea level, the less dense is the air. For example, there are fewer air molecules in a Denver kitchen than there are in a Seattle kitchen of the same size because Denver is very high above sea level. It takes less energy for an energized water molecule to jump out of the pan in Denver than it does in Seattle. At sea level, the boiling point is 100°C or 212°F. Water

7

in an open pan cannot get above its boiling temperature because when it does it ceases to be water and becomes steam instead.

In a closed pan such as the pressure cooker, water molecules absorb energy and escape into the air in the pan. However, since the pan is closed there is only limited space. Soon the air is packed with water molecules and no more space is available for steam. All of the steam molecules crowd into the air of the cooker and push down on the liquid. This push is called pressure. The energized molecules have no choice but to remain as a liquid and keep absorbing heat. Now the temperature of the water starts to heat up.

The weight on top of the valve allows air and then steam to escape when the pressure of the excited water molecules becomes too great. Most pressure gauges are set at 15 pounds. This means that the molecules in the vapor are pushing on the molecules in the liquid at 15 pounds of pressure. If the heat continues to rise, the pressure at which the vapor pushes down on the molecules in the liquid increases and lifts the gauge slightly off the valve, allowing steam to escape into the air and thereby equalizing the pressure.

Advantages of Pressure Cooking

Most cooks are attracted to the pressure cooker for the convenience it offers. Pressure cooking is quicker than cooking on a regular stove-top or oven and in some cases even quicker than the microwave. This makes it a must for two-career families and busy parents. And once high pressure is reached, the food does not have to be stirred, turned, or otherwise watched. Just set the timer, relax, and return when it goes off.

Pressure cooking is also an ideal cooking method for those concerned about nutrition. Foods prepared in the pressure cooker retain more vitamins than foods cooked by other means. The destruction of fat-soluble vitamins by oxygen is reduced because the steam drives most of the oxygen out of the sealed pan. In an open pan, water-soluble vitamins can be lost to the steam or boiling water. This does not happen in the pressure cooker where less water is used and steam does not escape. Food comes out lighter tasting and more heart healthful.

Pressure cooking seals the steam into the pot and unpleasant odors from foods like fish or cabbage are trapped. Flavors are not lost to the air either. And once the cooker reaches high pressure, only a small amount of heat is needed to keep the pot at that pressure. This produces less heat in the kitchen—a big help for hot-weather cooking.

The pressure cooker is a "green" appliance, meaning it uses less water and fuel, nonrenewable natural resources. Because of its small size it is perfect for camping trips, for use in recreational vehicles, boats, or for a dorm room.

And the pressure cooker is versatile. You can use it to make a whole meal or a single entrée, everything from hearty stews to delicate custards. Precooking foods by browning and steaming can be done in the pressure cooker and ingredients can be added or the dish can be thickened later.

The leanest cuts of meat are usually tough; they are also flavorful and cheap. Your pressure cooker can transform tough meats into fork-tender masterpieces. Tough cuts do not contain a lot of fat or marbling. What they contain are substantial amounts of tough connective tissue. When a tender cut of meat is cooked without the pressure cooker, the fat in between the muscle fibers melts and the meat appears juicy. When tough cuts are cooked in this manner, the heat cooks the connective tissue which makes it tough and difficult to chew. But if you pressure-cook this connective tissue, it turns into a soft gelatinous substance that makes meat tender and flavorful.

Root vegetables such as potatoes, sweet potatoes, yams, beet roots, turnips, and rutabagas take well to pressure cooking. Using conventional cooking methods, these roots and tubers can take 1 to 2 hours to cook, but with the pressure cooker can take 10 to 20 minutes.

Cooking time in the pressure cooker depends on the size of the pieces, not the number. A large pot roast will take longer to cook than the same cut of meat chopped into 1-inch cubes. And remember, the longer a food cooks the more water you need.

Pressure Steaming

You can pressure-steam foods using the trivet or steamer basket that came with your cooker. Many different foods can be steamed in your pressure cooker at the same time without flavors mingling. This works well with vegetables, seafood, and serving sizes of some meats. To steam foods follow these steps:

1. Fill the pan with the recommended amount of water.
2. Coat the trivet or steamer basket with nonstick spray and place it in the pan.
3. Put food in the steamer basket, making sure that the water does not touch the food and that the food does not touch the sides of the cooker.
4. Seal the lid on the cooker and turn the heat on high. For recipes cooked in wine or those with ingredients such as cranberries, oatmeal, or pastas that have a tendency to foam, bring to high pressure on medium heat.

   For pressure-steaming foods in containers, use only oven-proof glass, metal cups, or boilable plastic bowls and cook for an additional 4 to 6 minutes. Make sure that the highest point of the dish does not rise above the 2/3 mark.
5. When the pressure regulator starts to rock, hiss, or spin, turn the heat down and set your timer for the correct cooking time.
6. When the timer goes off, remove pressure cooker from heat. For quick-cooking recipes, particularly seafood and delicate vegetables, place the cooker immediately under cold running water until the pressure vent falls.
7. Take the lid off carefully and remove the whole basket with food.

Browning

To brown ingredients such as meat, onions, garlic, mushrooms, or leeks:

1. Coat the inside of the cooker with nonstick spray. You can use olive oil or your favorite oil, but remember this will add fat.

2. Place on medium heat and gently brown.
3. Remove the browned food, add water, and proceed as directed in recipies.

Pressure Cooking

You can use your pressure cooker without the steamer basket and place the food directly into the pan. By stewing or poaching the food in the liquid, flavors mingle during the cooking. The superheated steam shoots through the flavors and joins them together as if they had been cooking all day. To stew or poach foods:

1. Spray the inside of the pan with nonstick cooking spray (or coat with olive or canola oil, depending on your taste for fat).
2. If you are going to brown any ingredients, do that first.
3. Then add all the ingredients including adequate liquid.
4. Place lid tightly on cooker and turn heat on high.
5. When the pressure regulator starts to rock, hiss, or spin, turn the heat down and set your timer for the correct cooking time.
6. When the timer goes off, remove pressure cooker from heat. For recipes that contain large amounts of liquid, let the pressure fall on its own.
7. Take the lid off carefully. Remember, hot steam can burn. Remove food.
8. The liquid remaining from poaching can now be thickened and used as a sauce.

Releasing Pressure

When the food has been cooking for the recommended amount of time, reduce the pressure before removing the lid. Pressure can be reduced in three ways.

1. The *slow-release method* simply means you let the cooker sit there quietly until the pressure drops on its own. This is the recommended method for soups, stews, and some delicate desserts.

2. Some cookers have a *quick steam release button*. When you hold it down, steam shoots out. Make sure no fingers are in the path of the steam since it can burn. This method takes anywhere from 15 to 30 seconds. If your machine does not have a pressure release button or for some reason you do not want odors from the cooker (for example if you are cooking fish or cabbage) circulating in the house, use the last method.

3. The fastest, easiest, and safest method of pressure release is the *quick release under water*. Simply carry the lidded pressure cooker over to the sink and run cold water on it. Keep a couple of oven mitts around to help with this and make sure the sink is empty. In just a few seconds the pressure inside will fall. Then when you open the cooker, no odors will escape and no dangerous steam will accost you.

Helpful Hints

- The pressure cooker needs water to produce the steam. The larger the cooker, the more water you will need.
- Since some water is lost during cooking, add additional water if the recipe requires a long cooking time.
- When steaming foods before pressure cooking (as for steamed puddings) or when steaming foods with the pressure weight off, watch the cooker carefully. Water can steam away quickly.
- Before you start a recipe, add the recommended amount of water and turn on the range. The water will be heating while you assemble the recipe and will reach high pressure quicker when the lid is sealed.
- For most foods, bring the cooker up to high pressure quickly then turn down the heat to maintain the pressure.
- When cooking foods with a high percentage of water such as soups and stews, bring pressure up slowly and reduce pressure after cooking slowly. This will help prevent the liquids from spurting out the valve.

- When using wine as the poaching liquid, bring the pressure up slowly. This will prevent the wine from spitting out the top and catching fire. (We found this one out the hard way.)
- Reduce pressure quickly for foods that are easily overcooked such as vegetables, seafood, and fruits.
- Reduce pressure slowly for custards, steamed puddings, and cakes.
- If your pressure cooker has a steam-release valve, make sure your hand doesn't get in the way of the steam. Painful burns can result.

Do's and Don'ts

- Don't try to fry foods under pressure. The oil will not produce steam and will eventually catch fire.
- Don't cook pasta. Pasta needs time to rehydrate and pressure cooking will not speed up the process.
- When making stews and soups, don't fill the cooker over half full. This will prevent the liquids from boiling up and clogging the vent.
- When cooking large pieces of meat, don't let the cut go above the two-thirds mark.
- Don't use thick ingredients such as tomato paste or bottled cooking sauces in the pressure cooker. Thin them down with water before adding to the pot. Thick ingredients will cause the recipe to stick to the bottom of the pan and burn.
- Do feel free to experiment with your pressure cooker. Some of the best soups and stews our families ever ate came from over-cooking recipes we were developing.
- Do reduce pressure before removing the cover.
- Do read your instruction manual and follow your manufacturer's instructions.
- Do use only ovenproof casseroles and dishes. Others can melt in the superheated steam.
- Do be creative with cooking liquids. Wine, beer, porter, canned stocks, ciders, and juices all make wonderful additions. Use your imagination.

- Do use your cooker to brown meats before pressure-cooking. This will increase the flavor of the recipe.
- Do brown onions, garlic, leeks, scallions, and carrots before cooking to increase the depth of flavor.
- Do thicken cooking liquid for use as a gravy or sauce. Just add 1 teaspoon of arrowroot, cornstarch, or flour for every 1 cup of liquid. Heat with cover off until thickened.

CHAPTER 3

Common Questions and Answers

Some people are intimidated by pressure cookers because of the sound and noise they make. You don't have to be. A pressure cooker is one of the safest appliances you can have in your kitchen. This chapter will answer some of the most frequently asked questions about pressure cooking. Before long, your pressure cooker will be your best friend.

The Basics

How much time do pressure cookers really save? The time-saving is actually very dramatic. Pressure cookers are at least three times faster than normal cooking methods and are just about twice as fast as the microwave.

How old is the method of pressure cooking? The principles of superheated steaming in a sealed pot are almost three hundred years old, but American manufacturers have been making and selling pressure pots for use in the home for more than seventy years.

What kind of liquids are suitable for use in the pressure cooker? Any liquids that contain water. This includes wine, beer, stocks, and tomato and other vegetable and fruit juices.

Which liquids should I avoid using in the cooker? Do not use any liquid that does not contain water such as oils or oiled-based marinades and dressings. Milk and milk-based products should also be avoided as they have a tendency to boil over and foam. These liquids should be added after pressure cooking has been completed and the cooker is open.

Are there any foods I should not prepare in the cooker? Most manufacturers recommend against cooking applesauce, cranberries, rhubarb, split peas, pearl barley, oatmeal, soup mixes containing dried vegetables, or other cereals and pastas, including macaroni and spaghetti. These foods are likely to foam during cooking and clog the vent pipe.

Do I have to brown meat before pressure-cooking it? Browning does improve the appearance of some meats and increases the flavor of the recipe, but meat does not have to be browned before cooking and it does not seal in juices.

How can I cook meats with different cooking times together? Cooking time in the pressure cooker is determined partly by the size of the piece of meat. Cut longer-cooking pieces of meat into smaller pieces. This also applies to vegetables. Of course, you can always quick-cool the cooker and add quickly cooked foods near the end of the cooking period.

When do I start timing? Set your timer as soon as the pressure regulator begins to turn, hiss, or rock. Then reduce the heat until the pressure regulator turns, hisses, or rocks slowly. Remove the cooker from the heat as soon as the timer goes off.

What does rock or hiss slowly mean? This means that the regulator turns or rocks 1 to 4 times a minute. Any faster than that means you are wasting energy and losing steam.

What do I do if the food is not done cooking at the end of the recommended cooking time? Recover the cooker, bring it up to pressure again, and cook for a few minutes longer.

How can I tell when the pressure inside the cooker has fallen enough for me to remove the lid? The pressure regulator will stop moving and hissing then the air vent (lock cover) will fall. Never attempt to open your cooker until pressure has been released.

Common Problems

How can I prevent food from burning on the bottom of the cooker?

- Use a timer to accurately set cooking time.
- Use the largest burner on your range so that heat is distributed evenly over the bottom of the cooker.
- Use enough liquid to cover the entire bottom. At least 1 cup is necessary but you should follow the recommendations of your manufacturer.
- Use a medium to high heat setting to raise cooker to high pressure. Too low a temperature can cause the food to burn before reaching the proper pressure.
- Use low heat setting after cooker reaches pressure. Too high a flame will cause the steam to burn away.

How can I prevent food from sticking to the bottom of the cooker? Before adding the food, coat the bottom of the cooker with a nonstick spray (or lightly coat the bottom with oil). Thick mixtures such as chili sauces and tomato sauces burn easily. Thin them by adding water. After cooking, the food can be thickened again by reducing the mixture with the cover off or by adding a thickening agent such as cornstarch, arrowroot, or flour.

The recipe is too watery. What can I do? The pressure cooker needs a certain amount of water to generate the pressure. As a consequence, some recipes are on the diluted side when cooking is finished. Simmer the recipe in the open cooker to evaporate some of the excess water.

Troubleshooting

What is the problem when steam continually leaks out of the cover and pressure does not rise? It is normal for a small amount of steam to escape and form droplets around the lid and handles. If the leakage continues it could be because:

• the handles of the cooker are misaligned causing the cover lock not to seal,
• the lift pin opening is blocked with food particles,
• the gasket has shrunk and has not formed a seal,
• the rim of the cooker is dented (from banging spoons and so forth on cooker) and cannot form a seal.

Help, I can't get the cooker to open. The cooker may not open because the pressure is not fully down. This may be due to a clogged vent tube preventing pressure release. After the cooker has cooled, clean the vent pipe with a wire. The gasket in the lid could also be stuck to the rim of the cooker. This is the result of food bubbling up around the lid.

The cooking liquid spurts out of the valve tube. How can I prevent this? Do not fill your cooker more than two-thirds full. If liquids continue to bubble up, decrease the cooker volume by half or bring the pressure up on medium rather than high heat.

When do I need to replace the overpressure plug? The overpressure plug is a safety mechanism that allows pressure to escape in case the vent pipe becomes blocked. This plug will blow out when the pressure inside the cooker exceeds safety limits. If the overpressure plug blows, immediately cool the cooker. When completely cooled, remove the lid and clean out the vent pipe with a piece of wire.

Over time and with use, this pliable rubber plug may become hard and inflexible and unable to work as a pressure release valve. It should be replaced immediately. Once a plug has been blown out of the lid, it has served its purpose and cannot be used effectively again. Consult your owners manual on how to purchase a replacement.

When do I need to replace the gasket?

- When the smooth pliable gasket becomes hard and brittle or soft and sticky
- When steam is escaping around the rim of the cooker even though the vent pipe is clear and open
- When the gasket has become loose and stretched or shrunk

Maintenance

How do I clean the outside of my pressure cooker? Treat the outside of your cooker like any fine piece of aluminum cookware. Use a nonabrasive cleaner and sponge to remove burned-on food. Occasionally clean the exterior with a fine silver polish to renew its luster. Avoid the use of harsh scouring pads and abrasive cleaners that could dull the exterior.

What kind of cleaner should I use to clean the inside of my cooker? A simple solution of warm soapy water will do the trick in any cooker including the ones with nonstick linings. Do not use an abrasive cleaner as it will make fine scratches in the surface and may discolor the cooker. Always check to see that the vent pipe and air vent are clear. If blocked, use a skewer such as an unfolded paper clip to clear the openings under running water. The sealing gasket should be cleaned frequently.

What is the best way to clean a pressure cooker with burnt food in the bottom? If you burn food to the bottom of the pan, pour about 1/2 cup of baking soda and about 1 inch of water into the pan and boil it for a few minutes. The burnt food comes right off. Just use a scrub sponge or a brush to wipe out the bottom and it's clean.

What causes discolorations in my cooker and how can they be removed? Aluminum cookers can be discolored by iron and other minerals in the water and food. To remove these stains, add water to the cooker and 1 tablespoon of cream of tartar for each quart of water. Make sure the solution covers the discoloration. Cover the cooker, bring to high pressure, remove from heat, and let sit for 2 to 3 hours. Empty cooker and scour with steel wool pad, wash, rinse, and dry. An alternative method is to boil 1 part vinegar to 1 part water in the open cooker then wash, rinse, and dry.

Overheating the cooker can also cause varicolored stains called heat tints. These can be removed by using a copper or stainless steel cleaner.

PART II

The Recipes

Many of the recipes in the following chapters are made from just a few simple ingredients such as tomatoes, onions, olives, chicken broth, brown rice, olive oil, and Italian parsley. This is to simplify your week's shopping list and make for easier storage of foods to have on hand for quick meals.

To bring you flavors from around the world, we have also included some unusual flavorings such as lime leaves and coconut milk. Wherever an unusual ingredient is used, we assume most of you will have to venture out to a gourmet shop or deli to find it. So you don't make the trip for just one recipe, we have included them as optional in other recipes where they add an exceptional flavor combination. In this way you will have opportunities to use these ingredients again if you enjoyed them as much as we have. Spices are expensive if purchased in jars at chain grocery stores but surprisingly inexpensive if purchased from the bulk foods department at health food stores, co-ops, delis, gourmet shops, or from grocery stores that offer herbs and spices in bulk.

The pressure cooker is used in kitchens all over the world. In Japan, pressure cookers are used for fish, soups, beans, grains, and frequently in macrobiotic cooking for its healthful properties. In macrobiotic cooking there is an emphasis on retaining the moisture content of foods which helps food digest more easily. In India and Spain, where beans are the main source of protein and grains are cooked daily, the pressure cooker is invaluable. Again, pressure cookers are the main kitchen tool and used for preparing almost every meal. Indian fare is full of delicate spices such as cardamom, coconut, coriander, parsley, cloves, cinnamon, lime, and mint. The stronger spices such as curry and ginger work exceptionally well in the pressure cooker as they mingle under pressure with beans, rice, and vegetables. We have included some rich Indian dishes that are simple and easy to prepare.

The Mediterranean diet has become a part of many Americans' lives as more and more people are looking for a healthful balance of monounsaturated fats, fiber, vitamins, and minerals from whole foods. The basic ingredients in the Mediterranean diet are olive oil, tomatoes, and fresh vegetables including leafy greens, whole grains, onions, and spices. These foods lend themselves well to pressure cooker recipes and we have adapted our favorites here.

Remember, your finished meal will only be as good as the ingredients that went into it. Use the best produce, the freshest meat, and the most high-quality spices you can afford.

CHAPTER 4

Red Meat

Red meat comes from the muscle of animals and includes beef, veal, pork, lamb, and game such as rabbit and venison. Lean red meat is a good source of protein, iron, zinc, and vitamin B-12.

*P*ressure cooking is one of the best ways to prepare lean red meat. Your pressure cooker can transform a tough cut of meat into a flavorful, tender, lowfat delight. Pressure cooking also makes red meat more economical. Not only do leaner cuts cost less, but a little meat goes a long way when prepared in the pressure cooker.

Red meats are suited to stronger tasting seasonings than other types of food such as poultry and fish. Robust red wines, beer, and stout as well as garlic, onions, and hot peppers complement the hearty flavor of red meats. Cooking liquids can be reduced or thickened to make flavorful sauces and gravies or frozen for later use in soups or stews.

Tips for Cooking Meat

- Cook under high pressure or use the 15-pound weight.
- Be sure the cut of meat fits inside the cooker. At its highest point, the joint of meat should not rise above the two-thirds mark, which is usually stamped on the inside of the pot.

- Limit the size of round roasts to 3 pounds or less. Larger roasts will be done on the outside before they are tender in the middle.
- Brown meat and aromatic ingredients such as mushrooms, onions, and garlic before adding the cooking liquid. This will increase the flavor of the dish.
- Be creative with your cooking liquids. Beef has a hearty flavor and is suited for seasoning with red wine, beer, porter, broth, or tomato juice.
- Avoid thick ingredients that may stick to the bottom. If you want a thick sauce, dilute with water as you cook. Thin sauces can be reduced after cooking.
- Thicken sauces with cornstarch, arrowroot, or flour after cooking is completed.
- To brown frozen meat, let the cut defrost for 30 minutes, then brown as usual.

Nutrition Tips

- Choose a lean cut of meat. Lean cuts include unmarbled cuts of round, shank, tenderloin, sirloin, and center loin. Watch out for meat that is marbled; that means saturated fat.
- Trim all visible sources of fat before cooking. This will not only cut calories, it will help keep your heart healthy.
- You can further reduce the fat content of a recipe by leaving it overnight in the refrigerator. The fat will congeal on top and can be easily removed.
- Watch portion size. A serving size of beef is 3 ounces cooked or 4 ounces uncooked. This portion is only about the size of a deck of cards. A little beef goes a long way.
- When buying ground beef, choose extra lean that is no more than 16 percent fat by weight. The leaner you can find, the better.
- The protein in beef can increase the quality of vegetable protein. If you have concerns about the amount of protein in your diet, add small amounts of beef to bean and grain dishes.

Red Meat Timetable

MEAT	COOKING TIME
Beef	
Chuck roast, 3 pounds	35 minutes
Corned beef, 3 pounds	60 minutes
Beef liver, sliced	5 minutes*
Rolled rib roast, 3 pounds	30 minutes
Round steak, 1/4-inch thick	4 minutes*
Round steak, 1/2-inch thick	10 minutes*
Short ribs	25 minutes
Beef stew meat, 1-inch cubes	15 to 20 minutes
Game	
Rabbit, whole	12 to 15 minutes
Venison, 3 to 4 inches thick	30 to 40 minutes
Ham	
Ham slice, uncooked, 1-inch thick	9 to 12 minutes *
Ham slice, uncooked, 2-inch thick	12 to 20 minutes
Ham picnic shoulder, uncooked, 3 to 6 pounds	30 minutes
Ham shank, uncooked, 3 to 5 pounds	35 to 45 minutes
Lamb	
Lamb chops, 1/4-inch thick	2 minutes
Lamb chops, 1/2-inch thick	5 minutes
Leg of lamb, 3 pounds	35 to 45 minutes
Lamb stew meat, 1-inch cubes	10 minutes

continued on next page

Red Meat Timetable, continued

MEAT   COOKING TIME

Pork

Pork chops, 1/4-inch thick	2 minutes*
Pork chops, 1/2-inch thick	5 minutes*
Pork butt roast, 3 pounds	55 minutes
Pork loin roast, 3 pounds	60 minutes
Pork steak, 1/4-inch thick	2 minutes*
Pork steak, 1/2-inch thick	5 minutes*

Veal

Veal chop, 1/4-inch thick	2 minutes*
Veal chop, 1/2-inch thick	5 minutes*
Veal steak, 1-inch thick	10 minutes*
Veal roast, 3 pounds	45 minutes

* Quick cool

This timetable is for fresh or thawed meats only. Cook frozen beef, veal, and lamb for 25 minutes per pound and frozen pork for 30 minutes per pound. Cuts with a bone will require slightly more cooking time.

Pork Chops with Apples and Roots

The apples and sweet potatoes add just a touch of sweetness to the pork chops.

4 pork chops
2 cups baby carrots
1 cup small pearl onions
16 dried apple slices
8 small new red potatoes
2 large sweet potatoes
1 medium rutabaga, peeled and cut into quarters
1 1/2 cups nonfat chicken broth

Brown meat, carrots, and onions in cooker. Add remaining ingredients and cook 10 minutes. Let pressure fall on its own. Serve with steamed leafy greens such as kale, spinach, or bok choy.

Serves 4

Beef and Vegetable Casserole

This recipe has an unlimited number of variations. If time is a concern, thaw frozen roasts in the refrigerator all day.

3-pound pot roast
4 small carrots (about 1 cup)
1 cup sliced onions
1 cup water
1 cup dry red wine
4 medium potatoes
1 teaspoon salt
2 tablespoons vegetable bouillon
1 bay leaf

Coat cooker with nonstick spray and brown meat with carrots and onions. Add water, wine, potatoes, and seasonings. Cook 45 minutes on high pressure, then let pressure fall on its own.

Serves 4 to 6

Variations

Tomato Pot Roast

Add: 1 teaspoon oregeno and 1 teaspoon rosemary, or 2 teaspoons Italian seasoning

Add: 1 teaspoon (about 2 cloves) garlic, minced

Add: 1 can (16 ounces) stewed whole tomatoes, including juice

Reduce: water to 1/2 cup

Sweet Potato Pot Roast

Substitute: sweet potatoes for white potatoes

Substitute: 2 leeks (white part only) for onions

Substitute: 2 cups nonfat chicken broth for water and wine

Add: 8 slices dehydrated apple

Chili Pot Roast with Beans

Substitute: 1 cup dried kidney beans for potatoes

Substitute: 2 teaspoons chili powder for bay leaf

Substitute: 2 cans tomato juice for wine and water

Add: 1/4 teaspoon dried red pepper flakes

Add: 1 green pepper, chopped

Pineapple Pork with Honey Date Yams and Pearl Onion Peas

A complete dinner for two in only 15 minutes! This is an easy recipe that's a favorite at the Keane house.

2 pork steaks, trimmed of visible fat
2 yams
1 cup lowfat chicken broth
1 cup frozen pearl onions and peas mix
2 unsulfured dehydrated pineapple slices
Honey
Dried crushed dates (date sugar)

Coat cooker lightly with nonstick spray and brown meat. Slice yams almost, but not quite, all the way through so that the potato slices are held together. Add broth, yams, and frozen vegetable mix to browned steaks in cooker. Lay pineapple slices on top of steaks, bring to high pressure, and cook 10 minutes. Let pressure drop on its own. Before serving, drizzle honey on top of yams and sprinkle with dates.

Serves 2

Pot Roast with Onions and Root Vegetables

Fork-tender in only an hour! This easy-to-make recipe tastes like you have been lovingly watching over it all day! We particularly like the varied textures of the root vegetables.

3 pounds roast (chuck, loin, round, sirloin), trimmed of visible fat
2 to 4 tablespoons barbecue rub
2 onions, sliced into thick rings
1 cup burgundy wine
1 cup nonfat chicken broth
1 cup water
3 large carrots, cut into 1-inch slices
2 medium white potatoes, peeled and sliced
2 medium sweet potatoes, peeled and sliced
2 medium turnips, peeled and sliced

Trim roast of all visible fat and cover with barbecue rub. Coat cooker with nonstick spray and brown roast and half of the onions. Add liquids, bring to high pressure, and cook 50 minutes. Cool quickly under cold water and add the rest of the onions and the root vegetables. Bring to high pressure again and cook 10 more minutes. Quick cool.

Serves 6

Beaujolais Lamb

Other dry red wines can be substituted for beaujolais such as cabernet sauvignon, merlot, petite sirah, pinot noir, or zinfandel.

3 pounds leg of lamb, trimmed of visible fat
12 boiler onions
1 cup beaujolais
2 teaspoons fresh rosemary, or 1 teaspoon dried

Coat cooker with nonstick spray and brown meat and onions. Add wine and rosemary, bring to high pressure on medium heat, and cook 35 to 45 minutes. Let pressure fall on its own.

Serves 4

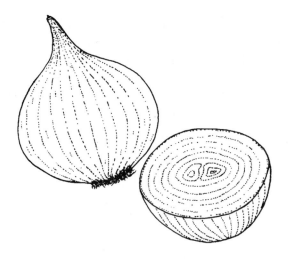

Beef and Black Beans

The kale in this recipe blends well with the meat and black beans.

1 ½ pounds boneless chuck, tip, or round
2 leeks, chopped
2 cloves garlic, crushed
2 cans (14.4 ounces each) chopped tomatoes with juice
1 ½ cups nonfat broth
1 can (14.5 ounces) black beans, rinsed and drained
2 cups kale, chopped
4 medium tomatoes, chopped
1 medium carrot, thinly sliced
2 tablespoons chopped fresh cilantro

Coat cooker with nonstick spray and brown meat, leeks, and garlic. Add the rest of the ingredients, except cilantro, bring to high pressure quickly, and cook for 30 minutes. Let pressure fall on its own. Add cilantro and serve.

Serves 4

Barbecue Steak with Maple Sweet Potatoes

An easy recipe for when you are on your own. You can substitute chicken for the beef; just reduce total cooking time to 10 minutes and cook the chicken along with the potato. When cooking for more than one, double the ingredients except for the water in cooker.

3 to 4 ounces lean round steak, trimmed of visible fat
2 tablespoons barbecue sauce
1 sweet potato or yam, scrubbed and sliced
1 to 2 teaspoons maple syrup or honey
1 tablespoon golden raisins
Cinnamon (optional)

Equipment
4 × 6-inch loaf pan
3 × 5-inch loaf pan
Trivet

Place metal rack in cooker and add 1 to 2 cups water. Place steak into larger pan and cover with barbecue sauce. Put pan on trivet, cover, bring to high pressure quickly, and cook 25 minutes.

While steak is cooking, line up potato slices in small pan. Drizzle maple syrup between slices and top with golden raisins.

Quick-cool cooker under cold water, remove steak, and place pan with yam into cooker. Bring again to high pressure, cook 10 minutes, and reduce pressure quickly.

Place steak on warmed dinner plate adding more barbecue sauce if desired. Turn small pan over on top of plate to unmold yam. Sprinkle top of yam lightly with cinnamon.

Serves 1

Hearty Beef and Barley Casserole

Kohlrabi is a member of the cabbage family but is milder in flavor. Look for it in the produce department of your grocery store. If you can't find kohlrabi, substitute cabbage or rutabaga.

1 pound lean stew beef, cut into 1/4- to 1/2-inch cubes
5 cups water
1 onion, diced
1 carrot, thinly sliced
1 leek, white part only, chopped into small pieces
1 large kohlrabi, peeled and chopped into small pieces
1/4 cup pearl barley
3 or 4 chicken or vegetable bouillon cubes
4 medium potatoes, boiled

Coat cooker with nonstick spray and brown meat, onion, and carrots. Add remaining ingredients except potatoes, bring to high pressure quickly, and cook 15 minutes. Let pressure drop on its own. Place one hot potato in each of four bowls and break with fork. Ladle stew into each bowl and serve with brown bread.

Serves 4

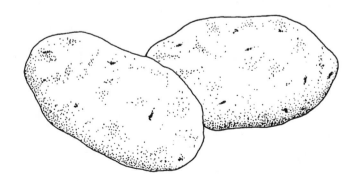

CHAPTER 5

Poultry

Poultry is the collective name for domesticated birds raised for their meat. It includes chicken, turkey, game hens, geese, pigeons, squabs, and duck. Pheasant and other game birds are also considered poultry. Poultry is an excellent source of lowfat protein, riboflavin, and niacin.

Chicken is one of the most popular meats in America. It is mild in flavor, tender in texture, low in fat, and cheaper than red meat. This makes it extremely versatile. Chicken can be prepared in any number of ways, limited only by your imagination. It is available in a variety of forms including fresh and frozen whole birds, parts, boneless skinless cuts, and ground meat. Turkey is also becoming popular and can now be found in as many guises as chicken.

Hint: When you pressure-cook a whole bird, save the cooking juices to use as stock for other recipes. Save the carcass, too. It can be added to some of the soup recipes later in the book.

Tips for Cooking Poultry

- Older birds such as stewing chicken, rooster, hen or tom turkey, and pigeon are more flavorful but less tender. These birds taste best when pressure-cooked.

- The length of cooking time is determined by the toughness of the meat and the size of the cut. For example, older chickens take longer to cook than younger ones and chicken parts take less time than a whole chicken.
- Remove the skin from poultry before cooking it. This will greatly reduce the amount of saturated fat and calories. And pressure-cooking shrivels the skin into an unappealing lump.
- Chicken without bones cooks faster than chicken with bones.
- Make sure that no part of the bird rises above the two-thirds mark.
- Poultry can be cooked fresh or frozen.
- Tie the legs to the bird with string or wrap the whole bird in cheesecloth. Pressure-cooking makes the meat so tender it will easily fall off the bird.
- Chicken can be browned before cooking or placed under the broiler to crisp after cooking is finished.
- Ground chicken or turkey is an excellent substitute for ground red meat. Because much of the juiciness of ground beef comes from its fat content, ground poultry can be dry. Adding filler will increase the moisture. Good fillers include oatmeal, beans, and bread crumbs.
- A whole chicken or turkey breast resembles a set of wings in size. A half chicken breast is the typical portion size.

Nutrition Tips

- Remove the skin and trim any visible fat from poultry to reduce saturated fat to a minimum.
- The white meat from the breast is lower in fat than the dark meat from the legs. However, the darker meat is often more flavorful.
- When buying ground poultry, make sure that it is made from skinless chicken. Poultry ground with skin on is very high in fat.
- Duck can be very fatty. To reduce the calorie count, cook the recipe, then cool in the refrigerator until the fat congeals on the top. Remove fat and reheat meat.

Poultry Timetable

Read your pressure cooker instruction manual to find the minimum amount of water the manufacturer of your machine recommends.

POULTRY	COOKING TIME AT HIGH PRESSURE
Chicken	
Whole, 4 to 5 pounds	25 to 30 minutes
Parts with bone, 3 pounds	9 to 11 minutes
Boneless parts, cut into pieces	2 minutes
Half breast with bone	10 to 12 minutes
Boneless half breast	3 to 5 minutes
Hindquarter, 1 to 2 pounds	10 to 15 minutes
Legs	8 minutes
Thighs	5 to 7 minutes
Frozen boneless thighs or breasts	5 to 7 minutes
Ground, 1 pound	2 to 3 minutes
Whole Cornish hen	8 to 10 minutes
Duck, cut into pieces	8 to 10 minutes
Pheasant, cut into pieces	7 to 10 minutes
Pigeon, halved	25 to 30 minutes
Turkey	
Parts, cut ino pieces	2 to 3 minutes
Legs	15 to 20 minutes
Half breast with bone	25 to 30 minutes
Boneless half breast	15 to 20 minutes
Hindquarter	25 to 30 minutes

Poached Chicken

Vary the poaching liquids and seasonings. We have listed wine here, but you can use tomato juice, vegetable broth, chicken broth, and other meat-based broths. Poached chicken can be topped with bottled spaghetti sauce or one of the sauces below. Do not use the trivet in this recipe.

4 half chicken breasts, boneless and skinless
3/4 cup dry white wine
3/4 cup water
1 teaspoon minced garlic (about 2 cloves)
1/4 teaspoon pepper
Salt to taste

Coat pan with nonstick spray. Add all ingredients and cook on high pressure for 10 minutes. Reduce pressure quickly and serve with one of the sauces that follow.

Poultry Sauces

Using nonfat or lowfat yogurt, sour cream, or mayonnaise keeps the fat and calorie content of your sauces down.

Confetti Sauce

1/2 cup yogurt
1/2 cup sour cream
2 tablespoons chopped green onions
2 tablespoons chopped red bell pepper
1 tablespoon chopped yellow bell pepper
1 tablespoon chopped green bell pepper

In a blender combine yogurt, sour cream, and onions. Pour sauce over hot chicken and sprinkle with chopped peppers.

Warm Curry Sauce

$^1/_2$ cup yogurt
$^1/_2$ cup mayonnaise
1 teaspoon curry powder
$^1/_2$ teaspoon prepared mustard

Combine ingredients in small pan and heat gently. Pour over hot chicken breasts.

Sour Cream and Dill Sauce

1 cup sour cream
2 teaspoons dried dill
1 tablespoon chopped onion

Combine ingredients and spoon over hot chicken.

Sherry Chicken with Garlic

This dish is excellent served with red wine and a fresh salad.

4 half chicken breasts
4 medium potatoes
1 cup dry sherry
1 tablespoon minced garlic (about 6 cloves)
10 cherry tomatoes
1/2 cup Italian parsley or basil leaves

Add all ingredients to the pan and cook under high pressure for 10 minutes. Quickly reduce pressure. Top chicken with halved cherry tomatoes, chopped fresh Italian parsley, or basil leaves.

Serves 4

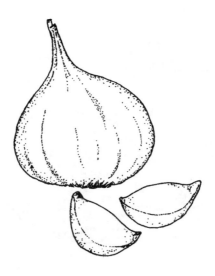

Two Can Turkey

A remarkably easy recipe. You can use any variety of the preseasoned canned tomatoes. If your store does not carry them, add 2 teaspoons of mixed herbs to unseasoned canned tomatoes.

1 turkey center loin, skinless and boneless, cut into 1-inch slices
1 can (16 ounces) seasoned tomatoes with juice
1 can (8 ounces) new potatoes with water

Combine all ingredients and cook on high pressure for 10 minutes. Reduce pressure under cold water and serve immediately.

Serves 2

Variations

Mexican-Style Turkey

Substitute: 1 can (16 ounces) Mexican-flavored tomatoes for unseasoned tomatoes

Substitute: 1 can (16 ounces) red kidney beans, drained, for potatoes

Add: ¹/₂ cup water

Italian Turkey Legs

Substitute: 1 can (16 ounces) plum tomatoes for unseasoned tomatoes

Add: 1 teaspoon Italian seasoning

Add: 3 cloves garlic (about 1 ¹/₂ teaspoons)

Poultry Casserole

Here is a basic recipe for creating poultry casseroles. Add your family's favorite vegetables and grains. This is always a good recipe for potluck suppers.

2 chicken legs, skinned
1 chicken breast, skinned and cut in half
2 chicken thighs, skinned
1 cup boiler onions
1 cup chicken broth
1 cup dry white wine
3 carrots, cut into 2-inch pieces
2 cups small red potatoes, cut in half
1/2 teaspoon pepper
1 bay leaf
Salt to taste
2 tablespoons arrowroot dissolved in 2 tablespoons water

Coat pan with nonstick spray and brown chicken parts with onions. Add all remaining ingredients, except arrowroot mixture, and bring to high pressure. Cook for 10 minutes and let pressure fall on its own. Open cooker, add arrowroot mixture, and cook until casserole reaches desired thickness.

Serves 6

Variations

Ginger Chicken

Substitute: 8 chicken thighs, skinless and boneless, for combination parts

Substitute: 1/2 cup dry sherry for white wine

Substitute: 1 cup chopped yellow onion for boiler onions

Substitute: 2 large sweet potatoes, cut into 2-inch slices, for red potatoes

Increase: chicken broth to 1 1/2 cups

Add: 1 tablespoon minced ginger root

Add: 2 teaspoons minced garlic (about 4 cloves)

Add: 1/4 cup soy sauce

Add: 1 tablespoon sesame seeds for garnish

Creamed Turkey Casserole

Substitute: 1 large half turkey breast, boneless, skinless, cut into 1-inch slices, for chicken

Substitute: 1 cup dry red wine for white wine

Substitute: 2 large carrots, sliced, for carrot pieces

Substitute: 2 large potatoes, cut into 3/4-inch slices, for red potatoes

Add: 1 medium zucchini, cut into 3/4-inch slices

Add: 1/3 cup yogurt (stir in after arrowroot has been added)

Coconut Curry Chicken

Chutney or fruit salad are the perfect accompaniments to this fabulous curry dish.

4 half chicken breasts, boneless and skinless
1 red onion, sliced
1 large green bell pepper, sliced
2 tablespoons minced garlic (about 6 cloves)
1 1/2 to 2 cups water
1 tablespoon fresh ginger root, finely chopped
1 tablespoon soy sauce

Coat cooker with nonstick spray and brown chicken with onion, bell pepper, and garlic. Add water, ginger root, and soy sauce, bring to high pressure, and cook for 10 minutes. Quick-cool under cold water. Remove chicken and vegetables and serve with generous amounts of sauce.

Serves 4

Sauce
1/2 cup unsweetened lowfat coconut milk
2 tablespoons curry powder
1 tablespoon soy sauce
2 teaspoons Chinese chili sauce (optional)
1 teaspoon hot chili sesame oil (optional)
1 tablespoon cornstarch mixed with 2 tablespoons cold water

Combine ingredients and mix well. Heat gently, stirring until thickened.

Hawaiian Chicken

Dried pineapple rings on top of the chicken give this dish a tropical flair.

4 half chicken breasts
1 1/2 cups dry sherry
8 dehydrated pineapple rings
1 tablespoon minced garlic (about 6 cloves)
1 tablespoon minced fresh ginger root
1 tablespoon soy sauce
1 tablespoon sesame seeds
2 tablespoons cornstarch dissolved in 1/4 cup water

Combine all ingredients except cornstarch mixture in pan and cook under high pressure for 10 minutes. Quickly reduce pressure. Remove chicken and pineapple and add cornstarch mixture. Heat sauce until thickened. Pour over chicken, top with pineapple slices, and serve with rice.

Serves 4

Chicken and Dumpling Casserole

A warm and comforting dish, serve it with a mound of fresh steamed vegetables.

8 chicken thighs, boneless and skinless
2 cups chicken broth
1 cup dry white wine
2 teaspoons minced garlic (about 4 cloves)
2 cups whole grain biscuit mix
2/3 cup skim milk
1 tablespoon dried dill

Add chicken thighs, broth, wine, and garlic to cooker and cook for 6 minutes under high pressure. Reduce pressure quickly under cold water. Combine biscuit mix, milk, and dill and drop large spoonfuls into boiling chicken broth. Cook uncovered for 6 minutes.

Serves 4

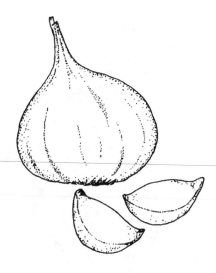

Tomato Turkey Breast with Rosemary and Oregano

This recipe is lowfat and full of flavor. We like it best when fresh herbs are used but dried herbs can be substituted. Substitute chicken breasts if you wish.

1 half turkey breast, boneless and skinless
1 cup chicken broth
2 cans (15 ounces each) chopped tomatoes with juice
1 tablespoon fresh rosemary leaves, finely chopped, or 1/2 tablespoon dried
1 tablespoon fresh oregano, finely chopped, or 1/2 tablespoon
   dried
1 tablespoon fresh cilantro, finely chopped, for garnish

Coat cooker lightly with nonstick spray and brown turkey breast. Add remaining ingredients, bring to high pressure, and cook for 15 minutes. Let pressure fall on its own. Remove turkey breast to a warm platter and reduce sauce over medium heat until tomatoes are no longer watery. Spoon tomatoes on either side of breast, sprinkle cilantro on top, and serve with brown rice pilaf, French-cut green beans, and a romaine salad.

Serves 2

Champagne Chicken with Shallot Sauce and Apple Rice

If champagne is not available, substitute any dry white wine such as chardonnay, sauvignon blanc, or chenin blanc.

4 half chicken breasts, boneless and skinless
1 1/2 cups instant brown rice, unseasoned
1 cup dry champagne
2 cups chicken broth
6 unsulfured dried apple rings
2 tablespoons sliced almonds
1/4 cup chopped shallots
1 tablespoon sliced almonds for garnish (optional)

Sauce
1 cup yogurt
2 tablespoons chopped shallots

Coat cooker with nonstick spray and brown chicken breasts. Add the rest of the ingredients, bring to high pressure, and cook for 10 minutes. While this is cooking, make the sauce by blending yogurt and shallots till smooth. Cool cooker quickly under cold water and serve breasts on top of rice. Pour about 1/4 cup sauce over each chicken breast and garnish with sliced almonds.

Serves 4

Hot Nutty Game Hens

This is an unexpected way to serve game hens. Pressure-cooking whole birds makes them so tender that the meat literally falls off the bone. To avoid this, tie the legs to the bird with string or cheesecloth. If you prefer a mild, more basic dish, omit chili powder, ginger, curry powder, and nuts.

3 Cornish game hens
1 onion, sliced
1 clove garlic, crushed
1 1/2 cups chicken broth
1 teaspoon chili powder
1 teaspoon ground ginger
1 tablespoon curry powder
3 tablespoons yogurt
1/4 cup cashew nuts

Equipment
Cheesecloth strip, about 12 inches by 6 inches

Coat cooker with nonstick spray and brown hens, onion, and garlic. Remove hens and tie cheesecloth strip around legs. Return wrapped hen to cooker and add broth, chili powder, ginger, and curry powder. Bring to high pressure, cook for 8 minutes, and reduce pressure quickly under cold water. Remove and unwrap hen. Boil to reduce cooking liquid by one third, remove from heat. Stir in yogurt and nuts just before serving.

Serves 3

CHAPTER 6

Seafood

Seafood includes fish, clams, crabs, lobster, mussels, shrimp, oysters, and scallops. Fish and shellfish are excellent sources of lowfat protein, niacin, iron, potassium, phosphorus, vitamin D, and omega-3 fatty acids. In the United States alone, over 50 species of fish and shellfish exist.

Most people are not aware of the benefits of pressure-cooking seafood. Since fish cooks so quickly by any method, why use the pressure cooker?

Less liquid is required. This means less dilution of flavor and better retention of vitamins and minerals. Odors from cooking fish are greatly reduced. It is also very easy to cook frozen fish in the pressure cooker. This makes it possible for the busy cook to keep fish in the freezer until it is needed.

Pressure cooking is best suited for thick pieces of fish like salmon and halibut steaks. Do not pressure-cook thin or delicate fillets such as sole and whitefish.

Tips for Cooking Seafood

- It is absolutely necessary to use a timer when cooking seafood. A few seconds can mean an overcooked rubbery mess instead of a tender, flavorful dish.

- Reduce pressure immediately for all seafood.
- To steam, use a well-oiled trivet and do not let the steaming liquid come into contact with the fish.
- To poach, do not use the trivet.
- Freeze the poaching liquid into cubes and store in freezer for later use in soups or sauces.
- Wash shellfish thoroughly with a brush.
- Discard any shellfish that have their shells open.

Nutrition Tips

- Fish are an excellent source of a particular kind of fat—omega-3 fatty acids. These fats are implicated in reducing inflammation and cell damage, reducing the stickiness of platelets in the blood (thereby decreasing the chances of a blood clot), and dilating blood vessels which helps reduce high blood pressure.
- By substituting fish for red meat, you can reduce the amount of total fat and saturated fat in your diet.
- When making sauces, be careful of the bases you use. Nonfat yogurt is always a good choice. Mayonnaise is only as healthful as the oil it is made with; choose canola oil-based mayo if you can. Remember, each tablespoon of oil contains 14 grams of fat and 125 calories.

Tips for Buying Seafood

- Buy only fresh fish. Fresh fish have bulging eyes, firmly adhering scales, and firm flesh.
- Never buy fish that has a bad odor. This is an indication that it has started to decay.
- Buy fish the day you are going to cook it. Store fish in the refrigerator for only a day.

- Only fresh fish can be stored in the freezer. If the fish you have bought has been frozen (usually, not always, indicated on the package), use it within 24 hours and do not refreeze.
- Choose clams and mussels with shells that are tightly closed. Partially or fully open shells can indicate an animal that is dead or stale.
- The flesh of fish is very easily digested by humans, but also by bacteria. For this reason, fish deteriorate rapidly and should always be stored properly.

Seafood Timetable

All seafood should be quick-cooled under cold water.

SEAFOOD	COOKING TIME AT HIGH PRESSURE (THAWED)
Clams	3 minutes
Crab legs	2 minutes
Fish fillets, 1-inch thick	2 minutes
Whole fish	5 to 6 minutes per pound
Lobster tail, 6 to 8 ounces	5 minutes
Lobster tail, 12 to 14 ounces	8 minutes
Salmon steak, 1-inch thick	2 minutes
Scallops, small	1 minute
Scallops, medium or large	2 minutes
Shrimp, small	1 minute
Shrimp, medium	2 minutes
Shrimp, large	3 minutes

Poached Fish with Julienned Vegetables

Use thick fillets of fish. Be careful not to overcook. Use a timer for best results.

½ cup dry white wine
½ cup water
4 fish fillets, thawed
1 cup shredded carrots
1 cup zucchini, cut into very thin strips
1 cup green beans, cut into very thin strips

Add wine, water, and fish to cooker and pile vegetables on top. Bring to high pressure quickly and cook for 3 minutes. Reduce pressure quickly under cold water. Serve fish with a dusting of dill or with one of the sauces that follow.

To pressure-steam fish, place fillets and vegetables on a well-oiled trivet and follow the directions above.

Serves 4

Seafood Sauces

Chipotle Cocktail Sauce

1 bottle (12 ounces) chili sauce
1 tablespoon finely minced, canned chipotle chiles in sauce
1 tablespoon freshly squeezed lime juice
1 teaspoon finely minced or grated lime zest
1 teaspoon finely minced or grated orange zest
1 teaspoon Worcestershire sauce

Combine all ingredients and mix well. Refrigerate until needed. This sauce can be prepared up to 5 days in advance.

Lemon-Tarragon Vinaigrette

1/4 cup freshly squeezed lemon juice
2 tablespoons white wine vinegar
2 tablespoons minced fresh tarragon, or 1 tablespoon dried
2 teaspoons minced shallot
1 teaspoon honey
1/2 teaspoon lemon zest
1/4 cup olive oil
Salt and pepper to taste

Combine all ingredients and serve. Store refrigerated for up to 3 days. This sauce is great drizzled over scallops or any white fish.

Basic Sauces

Seafood sauces have a reputation for being tricky to make and indulgently rich, but many are both easy and light on the fat. Here are just a few ideas for basic sauces that you can build and expand on.

Yogurt Sauces

For zesty flavor, add minced or grated ginger, minced or pressed garlic, chopped capers and/or minced fresh chiles to plain non-fat yogurt. Also consider adding onions that have been sautéed in olive oil with a generous seasoning of curry powder. More subtle additions are minced fresh herbs, chopped tomato, and ground cumin.

Mayonnaise Sauces

The rich quality of mayonnaise is a good base for sauces to serve with leaner, milder fish. Any of the seasonings mentioned for yogurt sauces can be used with mayonnaise. To modify the rich-ness of mayonnaise, add freshly squeezed lemon or lime juice, with grated zest if you like pronounced citrus flavor. Since mayonnaise is almost all oil, consider using a lowfat version and diluting it with nonfat yogurt. Or make your own mayonnaise using heart-healthful canola oil.

Vegetable Sauces

Vegetable sauces are particularly refreshing when made with raw, fresh ingredients—delicious with a wide variety of seafood. A familiar version is a salsa-like combination of chopped tomatoes with minced onion and minced herbs (cilantro, parsley, basil, oregano). Spiciness can be added with minced jalapeño, Tabasco, or dried red pepper flakes. Other ingredients to mix and match here include bell peppers, fennel bulb, celery, cucumber, and corn kernels. Season with salt and pepper, and a little vinegar, citrus juice, or olive oil if you like. Cooked vegetable sauces that you might serve on pasta dishes can also be delicious with fish.

Fruit Sauces

Fruit isn't a common sauce ingredient for seafood, but there are some tasty possibilities. A combination of minced tropical fruit (papaya, mango, pineapple) tossed with lime juice, chopped green onion, and minced mint or cilantro pairs surprisingly well with a fish fillet. Other fruits that taste good with fish are strawberries, oranges, bananas, kiwis, plums, and pink grapefruit. Fruits are rich in vitamin C and will enhance the absorption of iron from the seafood.

Vinaigrette Sauces

Good oil and good vinegar make a great sauce, especially for seafood. Add fresh herbs, green onions, capers, nuts, olives, garlic, mustard, crumbled feta or blue cheese—the possibilities really are endless. You can also use lemon or lime juice in place of vinegar for a thoroughly different type of vinaigrette. With richer, more full-flavored fish, use less oil than you might usually. Always whisk a vinaigrette sauce to thoroughly remix the ingredients just before spooning over the seafood.

Shrimp in Spicy Marinade

A wonderful party dish or appetizer.

1 ½ pounds large shrimp, peeled and deveined
1 ½ cups orange juice
1 teaspoon freshly squeezed lime or lemon juice
1 teaspoon finely minced or grated orange zest
1 teaspoon finely minced or grated lime zest
1 teaspoon ground cumin
1 teaspoon salt
1 teaspoon ground cinnamon
¼ teaspoon cayenne pepper
Lime wedges (for garnish)

Combine all ingredients in pressure cooker, bring to high pressure, and cook 1 minute. Remove from heat and let pressure fall on its own. Remove cover and cool 30 minutes. Cover cooker and chill shrimp and cooking liquid in cooker in refrigerator for 30 minutes. Remove shrimp from the liquid and scoop onto a serving platter or over ice. If desired, serve with chilled chipotle cocktail sauce with lime wedges.

Serves 4

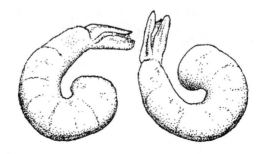

Lobster Steamed in Beer

The beer adds a very light accent to the lobster tails. Experiment with steaming other shellfish such as shrimp, crab, and clams in beer.

2 lobster tails
1 cup flat beer

Place beer and lobster into cooker and bring to high pressure over medium heat. Cook for 11 minutes and reduce pressure under cold water. Serve warm.

Serves 2

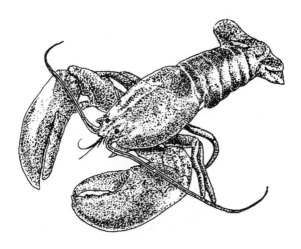

Steamed Clams

This recipe makes enough to feed two persons for a main course or 4 for an appetizer.

$^{1}/_{2}$ cup water
$^{1}/_{2}$ cup dry white wine
1 teaspoon minced garlic (about 2 cloves)
4 pounds clams
2 tablespoons cream

Combine water, wine, and garlic in cooker. Add clams, bring to high pressure on medium heat, cook 3 to 4 minutes, and reduce pressure quickly under cold water. Remove clams and boil to reduce broth. Add cream to clam juices and heat gently. Place clams in bowls and spoon sauce over them.

Serves 2

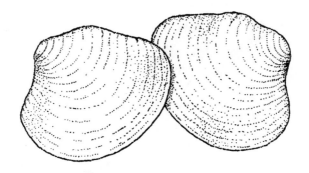

Orange Roughy with Mango

Try this dish with a combination of fruits such as papaya and pineapple or strawberries and kiwi.

2 orange roughy fillets
1 ripe mango, minced
3 green onions, chopped (about 3 tablespoons)
2 tablespoons lime juice

Equipment
Trivet, well-oiled

Add water to cooker and place trivet inside. Lay fish on trivet, bring to high pressure, and cook fish under pressure for 2 minutes. Cool quickly under cold water, remove fillets, and serve with mango, green onions, and lime juice.

Serves 2

Whole Fish in Red Curry Sauce with Lime Leaves

Red curry paste is not curry at all but a paste of red chili peppers and it is hot!

1 cup water
1 white-fleshed whole fish
1 tablespoon fish sauce
1 teaspoon red curry paste
1 teaspoon honey
1 fresh red chili, seeded and finely sliced
6 dried kaffir lime leaves (soaked for 10 minutes and sliced)
1/2 cup skim milk
1/2 cup lowfat coconut milk
Fresh coriander, basil, lemon wedges, sliced cucumbers and/or
    tomato slices for garnish

Equipment
Trivet, well-oiled

Add water to cooker and place trivet inside. Lay fish on trivet, bring to high pressure, and cook for approximately 5 minutes per pound. Cool quickly under cold water and remove fish from pressure cooker. Use pressure cooker to make curry sauce. Add all ingredients except coconut milk, bring to high pressure, and cook for 2 minutes. Reduce pressure quickly and remove lid. Add coconut milk and serve over fish.

Serves 4

Fish and Eggplant Curry

Use any type of fish with this recipe and it will turn out fabulous. The curry and lime leaves are the stars of this dish.

2 tablespoons red curry paste
1 tablespoon dried kaffir lime leaves (soaked for 10 minutes and sliced)
4 white-fleshed fish fillets, chopped
2 tablespoons fish sauce
1 eggplant, chopped
1 tablespoon whole basil leaves, or 2 teaspoons dried
1 cup skim milk
1 cup lowfat coconut milk

Add everything except coconut milk to pressure cooker and bring up to pressure. Cook under pressure for 5 minutes. Reduce pressure, add coconut milk, and serve.

Serves 4

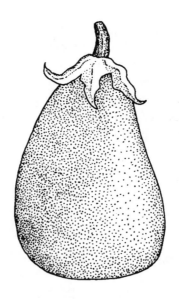

CHAPTER 7

Soups

The pressure cooker excels at making incredibly delicious soups. The superheated water mingles the flavors of the meats, vegetables, herbs, and seasonings, making them taste like they have been slowly cooking for hours. But it does all this in just minutes. It is almost as easy as opening a can of soup.

When making soups, it is important to keep the size of your pressure cooker in mind. The maximum amount of liquid in soups should be no more than three quarters of its capacity. If you have a 4-quart cooker, that translates into no more than 3 quarts or 12 cups. If the recipe contains grains (especially pearl barley), split peas, oatmeal, or any ingredient that expands when it cooks or has a tendency to foam, fill the cooker no more than half full. In a 4-quart cooker, 2 quarts or 8 cups; in a 6-quart cooker, 3 quarts or 12 cups.

Tips for Cooking Soup

- To make lowfat creamy soups substitute nonfat plain yogurt or lowfat sour cream for cream. Or pour half of the cooked vegetables into a blender, puree, and then add back to soup.

- Use fresh or canned juices for cooking liquids. Wine is also a good choice.
- Avoid adding thick ingredients before cooking. They can stick to the bottom of the pan and burn.
- Thicken soups with arrowroot, cornstarch, or flour after cooking or reduce the amount of liquid by cooking with the lid off.
- Presoak dried vegetables overnight or during the day, before cooking in pressure cooker.
- To add extra flavor, add canned broths, bouillon cubes, or powdered bouillon. We like to use a vegetable base that comes as a powder. You can find organic, low-sodium, natural seasonings in the health food department of your supermarket or in your local health food store.
- For best results, do not thicken foods before freezing.
- Don't throw away that turkey or chicken carcass. Toss it in the pressure cooker to make soup.

Nutrition Tips

- If you want to lose weight, soup can help decrease your appetite. Just make sure the ingredients are lowfat.
- To reduce the fat in soups, trim any visible fat off meats. Do not add cream to the finished soup. If possible, let soup sit overnight in fridge. The fat will rise to the top and congeal on the surface where it is easily removed.
- Soup is a great over-the-counter medicine. It can relieve stuffy sinuses and provide your body with the liquids it needs during illness.
- Remember to add lots of garlic or onions. These members of the Allium family have antibiotic properties that will not only make you feel better but can also help your immune system throw off a cold.

Soup Timetable

	MAXIMUM CAPACITY			COOKING TIME AT HIGH PRESSURE
	4-qt cooker	6-qt cooker	8-qt cooker	
Beef	8 to 12 cups	12 to 16 cups	16 to 20 cups	60 minutes
Chicken	8 to 12 cups	12 to 16 cups	16 to 20 cups	30 to 35 minutes
Fish	8 to 12 cups	12 to 16 cups	16 to 20 cups	15 to 20 minutes
Ham	8 to 12 cups	12 to 16 cups	16 to 20 cups	45 minutes
Grains	8 cups	12 cups	16 cups	15 to 60 minutes
Beans				
Presoaked	8 cups	12 cups	16 cups	20 minutes
Precooked	8 cups	12 cups	16 cups	10 minutes

Stock

Stock is the basis for soups, stews, gravies, and sauces. Traditionally it is made by simmering bones and meat for hours to extract their flavor. With the pressure cooker, these hours are changed to minutes without loss of any flavor.

These are perfect recipes to stash in your freezer. Get creative and add your favorite spices, herbs, and vegetables. You can cook multiple batches and store them in the freezer for up to 6 months. Strain stock by pouring through a sieve or colander. To freeze, pour the finished stock into plastic containers and cool in refrigerator

If you want to make a stock and the amount of food is greater than your cooker can handle, decrease the amount of water in the recipe and make a concentrated stock that can be diluted later. This is better than making a weak stock that has to be reduced.

Stock should not be salted. Only add salt when seasoning the final recipe.

Beef Stock

2 pounds meaty soup bones
1 medium yellow onion, chopped
2 carrots, sliced
3 cups water
1 cup dry red wine
2 bay leaves
2 ribs celery with leaves, chopped
4 peppercorns
1 teaspoon olive oil (optional)

Coat pan with nonstick spray and brown meat, onions, and carrots. Add the remaining ingredients, cover, and bring cooker to high pressure using medium heat. Cook for 20 minutes, letting the pressure fall on its own. Strain, cool in refrigerator, and remove the congealed fat from the surface. Use stock within the next few days or store in freezer.

Yields about 4 cups

Chicken Stock

3 pounds chicken backs, wings, and neck
1 medium yellow onion, chopped
2 carrots, sliced
4 cups water
2 bay leaves
2 ribs celery with leaves, chopped
1 teaspoon olive oil (optional)

Coat pan with nonstick spray and brown chicken, onions, and carrots. Add the remaining ingredients, cover, and bring cooker to high pressure using medium heat. Cook for 20 minutes, letting the pressure fall on its own. Strain, cool in refrigerator, and remove the congealed fat from the surface. Use broth within the next few days or store in freezer.

Yields 4 cups

Vegetable Broth

2 yellow onions, chopped
4 tablespoons minced garlic (about 6 cloves)
2 leeks, chopped
2 carrots, chopped
3 cups water
1 cup dry white wine
1/4 cup soy sauce
1 tablespoon fresh thyme, chopped, or 1 1/2 teaspoons dried
1/2 teaspoon ground cloves
2 ribs celery, chopped
1 fennel bulb with leafy green tops, chopped
1 (3-inch) cinnamon stick

Coat pan with nonstick spray and brown onions, garlic, leeks, and carrots. Add remaining ingredients, cover, and bring cooker to high pressure using medium heat. Cook for 20 minutes, letting the pressure fall on its own. Strain and cool in refrigerator. Use broth within the next few days or store in freezer.

Serves 8

Almost Instant Soup

Do not be afraid to experiment with a variety of cooking liquids and vegetables. Alternate ingredients are listed in parentheses.

1 cup boneless skinless chicken breast, chopped into 1-inch
    pieces
1 carrot, chopped (or 1 parsnip, chopped)
1 medium onion, chopped (or 1 leek, chopped)
3 cups water (or 2 cups water plus 1 cup white wine)
1 rib celery, chopped
1 bay leaf (remove after cooking)
6 peppercorns (remove after cooking)
Salt to taste

Coat pan with nonstick spray and brown meat, carrots, and onions. Add the rest of the ingredients and cook on high pressure for 12 minutes. Let pressure fall on its own.

Serves 6

Variations

Chicken Garlic Soup with Greens

Substitute: 2 to 3 teaspoons minced garlic (about 4 to 6 cloves) for onions

Add: 1 cup chopped greens. Spinach, kale, or collards work well. Just add the chopped greens after the cover has been removed and continue cooking without pressure until the greens are slightly wilted.

Beef Noodle Soup

Substitute: 1 cup boneless beef, chopped into 1/4- to 1/2-inch cubes

Substitute: 1 cup dry red wine for 1 cup water

Add: 1 cup noodles. Add noodles after the cover has been removed and continue cooking without pressure until the noodles are tender (5 to 7 minutes).

Chunky Chicken Soup

Substitute: 1 cup dry white wine for 1 cup water

Add: 1 cup baby red potatoes, quartered

Add: 1 cup coarsely chopped tomato

Add: 1/2 cup frozen peas

Ham and Bean Soup

Substitute: nonfat chicken broth for all of the water

Substitute: chopped cooked ham trimmed of fat, for the chicken

Add: 1 cup cooked kidney beans

European Pea Soup

The smoky flavor and hearty texture make this a perfect winter warmup.

1 tablespoon minced garlic
1/2 large onion, chopped
1/4 pound smoked lowfat ham, chopped
3 1/2 cups nonfat chicken broth
2 tablespoons chopped cilantro
1 carrot, finely chopped
1/4 pound split peas
1/4 teaspoon minced fresh ginger

Coat pan with nonstick spray and brown garlic, onions, and ham. Add remaining ingredients, bring to high pressure, and cook for 9 minutes. Let pressure fall on its own.

Serves 6

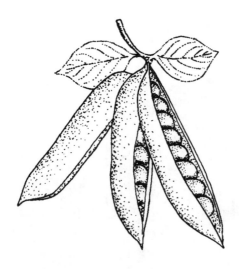

Beef Borscht with Sour Cream and Dill

This dish can be made vegetarian by leaving out the beef and using water or a vegetable broth in place of the beef broth. Use lowfat or nonfat sour cream or yogurt.

2 pounds sirloin steak, cut into 1-inch pieces
2 large onions, chopped
4 cups green cabbage, chopped
3 stalks celery, chopped
2 large carrots, chopped
4 cans (14 1/2 ounces each) lowfat beef broth
2 cans (14 1/2 ounces each) diced peeled tomatoes, with juice
4 large red potatoes, chopped
2 cans (16 ounces each) julienned beets, with juices
2 tablespoons cider vinegar
1 tablespoon sugar
6 tablespoons sour cream or yogurt
6 teaspoons chopped fresh dill

Coat pan with nonstick spray and brown steak, onions, cabbage, celery, and carrots. Add beef broth, tomatoes, and potatoes and cook under high pressure for 15 minutes. Quick-cool. Add beets, vinegar, and sugar and cook without lid to heat through. Serve with a dollop of sour cream and a sprinkle of dill.

Serves 6

Chicken Soup

This soup thickens naturally from the barley. We like to use un-hulled barley since it foams less than pearl barley and has a better texture and flavor.

2 medium onions, chopped
2 cloves garlic, minced
1 leek, chopped
5 cups water
1 cup unhulled barley
2 half chicken breasts with bone attached, skin removed
2 ribs celery, chopped
2 carrots, chopped
1 large potato, chopped
2 tablespoons soy sauce

Coat pan with nonstick spray and brown onions, garlic, and leek. Add remaining ingredients, bring to high pressure, and cook for 25 minutes. Let pressure fall on its own. Remove chicken bones and serve. If chicken is frozen, cook for an additional 5 minutes.

Serves 6

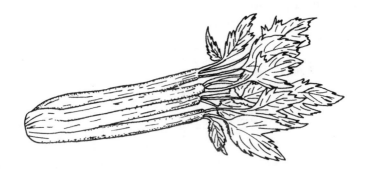

New England Clam Chowder

Use thinly sliced Black Forest deli ham for a delicate and lower fat version of this old favorite. The fat can be reduced further by substituting nonfat milk for lowfat.

1/2 pound lean sliced deli ham, cut into 1-inch pieces
1 medium onion, chopped
3 uncooked potatoes, cut into 1/2-inch cubes
1 can (16 ounces) corn, drained, liquid reserved
1 bay leaf
4 cups lowfat milk
4 cans (10.5 ounces each) minced clams, drained, liquid reserved

Coat pan with nonstick spray and brown ham and onions. Pour reserved liquid from clams and corn into a measuring cup and add enough water to this liquid to make 4 cups. Add this mixture to cooker along with the potatoes, corn, and bay leaf and cook under high pressure for 10 minutes. Quick-cool under cold water. Add milk and clams and heat *gently*, being careful not to boil. Remove bay leaf and season to taste.

Serves 6

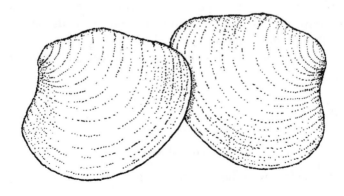

Seafood and Saffron Soup

This wonderful soup just needs some crusty bread to make it a meal. Be careful not to overcook the fish! Cooking fish too long will make it tough.

2 carrots, chopped
3 tablespoons minced garlic
1 large yellow onion, chopped
2 1/2 cups water
2 cups dry white wine
2 fennel bulbs, whole
1 (2-inch) piece fresh orange peel, washed thoroughly
1 cup Italian parsley, stemmed and chopped
3 bay leaves
2 tablespoons fresh thyme, chopped, or 1 tablespoon dried
1 tablespoon red pepper flakes
2 teaspoons freshly ground black pepper
1/2 teaspoon saffron threads
Salt and pepper to taste
1 pound cod or any white fish
1 pound medium-large shrimp (about 25)
1 pound scallops

Coat cooker with nonstick spray. Brown carrots, garlic, and onions, then add water, wine, fennel, seasonings, and cook under high pressure for 10 minutes, letting pressure fall on its own. Add fish, shrimp, and scallops and cook under high pressure for 3 minutes, then quick-cool. Remove bay leaves and serve with croutons.

Serves 8

Variation

Add: 5 lime leaves to the cooker for a fresh Thai flavor.

Hearty Multibean Soup

Use the leanest ground beef that you can find. We used 9 percent ground beef but choose beef that is no more than 16 percent fat by weight.

1 pound lean ground beef
1 medium onion, finely chopped
6 cups water or nonfat broth
1 cup cooked cannellini, or canned small white beans, drained
1 cup lentils (no need to presoak or cook)
1/4 cup tomato puree
1 can chick-peas, drained
1 teaspoon cloves
1 teaspoon hot red pepper flakes
1 teaspoon dried mint, crumbled
1 teaspoon ground pepper
Salt to taste

Coat pan with nonstick spray and brown beef and onion. Add remaining ingredients, bring to high pressure on medium heat, and cook for 20 minutes. Let pressure fall on its own.

Serves 10

Variations

Add: 1/2 cup bulgur

Add: 1/2 teaspoon chili powder

Add: fresh hot chili peppers, chopped

Minestrone

A soup that almost contains the entire food pyramid. Serve with some crusty bread to make a warm comforting meal. This is a large recipe that can be reduced by half. We recommend that you stash part of it in the freezer for those days when you are just too tired to cook.

5 stalks celery, chopped
3 carrots, chopped
1 large onion, chopped
2 tablespoons minced garlic
2 potatoes, chopped
2 tomatoes, chopped
1 zucchini, chopped
1 pound green beans
8 cups water
1 cup cooked white navy beans
1/2 cup whole wheat pasta (elbow macaroni)
1 tablespoon dried basil, or 1/4 cup fresh
2 additional tablespoons minced garlic
2 tablespoons grated parmesan or asiago cheese as garnish

Coat pan with nonstick spray and brown celery, carrots, onion, and garlic. Add remaining vegetables and water, bring to high pressure on medium heat, and cook for 5 minutes. Let pressure fall on its own. Open cooker and add cooked beans and pasta and boil for 10 minutes with top off. In blender, process basil, garlic cloves, and 1 cup soup from pot. After blending, return mixture to pot and stir. Garnish with cheese.

Serves 10

Onion Soup

This is a Parisian version of onion soup, gilded with a crust of bubbling cheese. It warms the belly and the delights the palate. Serve with a crusty whole wheat bread.

1 pound lean beef, cut into 1-inch cubes
2 medium onions, sliced
8 cups water
1 cup port
1 tablespoon dried bay leaves
1 teaspoon Worcestershire sauce (optional)
6 large onions, chopped
2 cubes beef bouillon
1 teaspoon salt
Crusty bread or croutons
8 tablespoons shredded Gruyère cheese

Coat pan with nonstick spray and brown beef and sliced onions. Add remaining ingredients, except cheese and bread, and cook under high pressure for 30 minutes. Let pressure fall on its own. Serve in deep bowls with a piece of bread or a few croutons on top and sprinkle with cheese. Place bowls under broiler until cheese melts and starts to brown. Remove and serve.

Serves 8

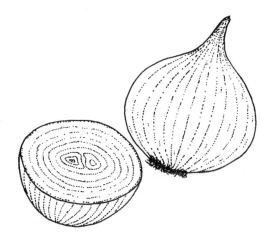

Beer and Bacon Bean Soup

Even if you don't like beer, you may take a liking to this peppery
bean soup. We have used lowfat Canadian bacon instead of the
highfat American version; you could also use lean ham.

1 large yellow onion, chopped
½ pound Canadian bacon, chopped
2 cups quick-soaked cannellini beans, drained
1 can Italian plum tomatoes, drained and chopped
5 ribs celery with leaves, chopped
2 anaheim peppers, chopped
1 tablespoon minced garlic (about 6 cloves)
1 bay leaf
Salt to taste
1 teaspoon freshly ground pepper
1 pint bottle beer, light or dark
1 cup broth or water

Coat cooker with nonstick spray and brown onion and bacon in
pressure cooker. Add remaining ingredients except for the beer
and broth. Pour in enough beer to cover the other ingredients
completely, add water or broth, bring to high pressure, and cook
for 35 minutes. Remove bay leaf and serve.

Serves 6

White Bean Soup

Take precautions handling chili peppers. Be careful not to touch
your eyes, mouth, or nose when working with them. Wash
hands well with soap after cutting or use latex gloves.

2 tablespoons minced garlic
2 large onions, thinly sliced
6 cups chicken broth
2 cups quick-soaked dried white beans (navy or cannellini)
6 stalks celery, with tops and leaves, chopped
1/2 pound carrots, sliced
1 sweet red bell pepper, sliced
1 small fresh chili pepper, thinly sliced
1 clove
1 bay leaf

Coat cooker with nonstick spray and brown garlic and onions.
Add all ingredients, bring to high pressure, and cook for 12 minutes. Let pressure fall on its own. Remove bay leaf and serve.

Serves 6

French Navy Bean Soup

The smoky flavor from the Black Forest ham adds depth to this hearty soup. Black Forest or lean Canadian bacon has only about 3 grams of fat per serving while American bacon has over 9 grams of fat per serving.

8 cups water or broth
3 cups quick-soaked French navy beans
1 pound Black Forest ham, chopped
3 ribs celery with leaves, chopped
2 carrots, chopped
1 large onion, chopped
2 tablespoons minced garlic (about 12 cloves)
1 tablespoon dried basil
1/2 teaspoon ground cloves

Add all ingredients to cooker, bring to high pressure, and cook for 45 minutes. Let pressure drop on its own.

Serves 6

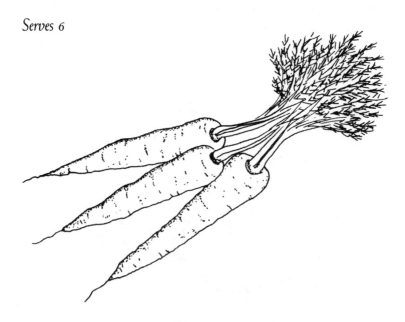

Cannellini Beans and Swiss Chard Soup

Swiss chard is actually a beet that has been encouraged by plant breeders to produce large leaves and fleshy stalks. The leaves have a full flavorful taste and are packed with beta carotene, vitamin C, potassium, and fiber.

1/2 pound extra-lean stew meat, cut into 1/2-inch pieces
1 yellow onion, coarsely chopped
2 tablespoons crushed garlic (about 12 cloves)
4 cups nonfat chicken broth
4 cups quick-soaked cannellini beans
2 cups Swiss chard, chopped
3 ribs celery, chopped
2 carrots, chopped
2 bay leaves
1 new red potato, chopped
Salt and pepper to taste

Coat pan with nonstick spray and brown meat, onion, and garlic. Add remaining ingredients, bring to high pressure on medium heat, and cook for 20 minutes. Remove bay leaves and serve.

Serves 6

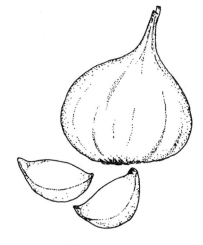

CHAPTER 8

Stews

The pressure cooker is perfect for making flavorful mouth-watering stews. Pressure cooking tenderizers the meat and infuses the flavors of the cooking liquid, spices, and herbs all through the stew. Absolutely anything can be thrown into a stew, even leftovers. When we make stews, no two are ever alike. What goes into the pot happens to be what's in the refrigerator that day.

Tips for Cooking Stews

- Never fill the cooker more than two-thirds full. Food can bubble up and clog the vent pipe.
- Brown aromatic ingredients before adding cooking liquid. It will intensify the flavor.
- Brown meats first. It will cause the browning reaction which creates flavors out of the proteins and sugars. If you are using frozen meat, allow it to thaw for 30 minutes so that you can still brown the surface.

- Do not thicken stew before cooking. It will burn and stick to the bottom of the pan.
- The size of the ingredients determines cooking time. If you would like to make a stew with two meats that have different cooking times, cut one of them into smaller pieces.
- If you like your vegetables not too well done, add them halfway through the cooking process.

Nutrition Tips

- Stews are great places to "hide" vegetables. If your child will not eat carrots, for instance, cut them into very small pieces and they will disappear into the surrounding stew.
- Add vegetable juices to stews to increase their nutritional value.
- If you would like to decrease your family's consumption of red meat, add more vegetables to the stew and less meat.

Lamb Stew

A nice change from beef. You can substitute wine for part of the broth.

1 pound lamb stew meat, cut into 1/2-inch cubes
2 medium onions, chopped
3 1/2 cups nonfat chicken broth
1 teaspoon Worcestershire sauce
1 teaspoon dried rosemary
1 teaspoon dried thyme
Black pepper to taste
5 medium potatoes, sliced
3 carrots, sliced
1 bay leaf
2 tablespoons Arrowroot dissolved in 2 ounces cold water
Salt to taste

Coat cooker with nonstick spray and brown meat and onions. Add broth and seasonings and bring to high pressure on medium heat. Cook for 6 minutes. Quick-cool cooker under cold water and add vegetables. Bring pressure back up to high and cook another 3 minutes. Quick-cool. Remove bay leaf, add arrowroot mixture, and heat until thickened. Add salt to taste. Serve with dumplings and a green salad.

Serves 4

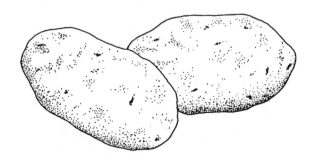

Quick Beef Stew

This quick recipe will taste like it's been simmering on the back of your stove all day long.

1 pound lean stew beef, cut into 1-inch cubes
1 medium onion, chopped
2 cups beef broth
1 1/2 cups burgundy
1 bay leaf
1/2 teaspoon basil
1/2 teaspoon garlic powder
4 medium potatoes, cut into cubes
3 carrots, cut into 1-inch slices
1 cup sliced celery
2 tablespoons arrowroot dissolved in 2 ounces cold water
Salt to taste
Coat cooker with nonstick spray and brown meat and onions. Add broth, wine, and seasonings, bring to high pressure on medium heat, and cook for 6 minutes. Quick-cool cooker under water, open, and add vegetables. Again bring to high pressure and cook another 3 minutes. Quick-cool. Remove bay leaf and add arrowroot mixture. Heat until thickened. Add salt to taste. Serve with dumplings and a green salad.

Serves 4

Variations

Beef and Bean Stew
Reduce: stew beef to 1/2 pound
Omit: potatoes
Substitute: chili powder for garlic powder
Substitute: 2 medium tomatoes, chopped, for carrots

Add: 1 cup canned red kidney beans, drained, along with other vegetables

Add: pinch crushed red pepper

Add: 1 green bell pepper, diced

Chicken Stew

Substitute: 1 pound boneless skinless chicken thighs and breast, for beef

Substitute: dry white wine for burgundy

Substitute: button mushrooms for celery

Substitute: leeks for carrots

Turkey-Vegetable Stew

Substitute: turkey breast for beef

Reduce: 4 potatoes to 2 potatoes

Substitute: 2 peeled sweet potatoes for 3 carrots

Substitute: dry white wine for burgundy

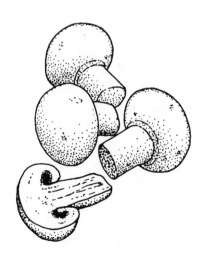

Chicken and Chick-pea Stew

We like to serve this stew over rice with cilantro, sesame seeds, and lemon juice sprinkled on top.

2 pounds boneless, skinless chicken breasts, cut into cubes
2 yellow onions, sliced
2 tablespoons chopped garlic (about 6 cloves)
2 cups cooked chick-peas, or 1 can (15 ounces), drained
1 can (28 ounces) Italian plum tomatoes with juice
1 eggplant, chopped
1 teaspoon cumin
1 teaspoon allspice
1 teaspoon turmeric powder
1/2 cup water or broth

Coat cooker with nonstick spray and brown chicken, onions, and garlic. Add the remaining ingredients, bring to high pressure quickly, and cook for 3 minutes. Let pressure fall on its own.

Serves 4

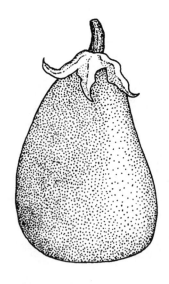

Spicy Vegetable Bean Stew

New Mexico green or red chilies are also known as California green or red chilies, chiles verde and Chiles Colorado. This is the familiar pepper that, when dried, makes up the popular, bright string or wreath called a *ristra*. These peppers are widely available fresh, canned, or dried.

2 medium yellow onions, chopped
1 tablespoon chopped garlic (about 6 cloves)
5 1/2 cups chicken broth
2 cups chopped Swiss chard
1 cup dried chick-peas, soaked overnight
1 cup dried cannellini beans, soaked overnight
1/4 cup tomato puree
2 carrots, chopped
2 white turnips, chopped
1 fresh New Mexico chili, chopped

Coat cooker with nonstick spray and brown onions and garlic. Add remaining ingredients, bring to high pressure, and cook for 25 minutes. Let pressure fall on its own.

Serves 10

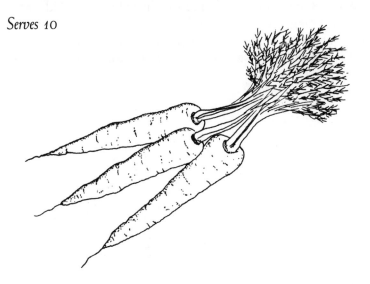

Moroccan Bean and Rice Stew

Dried chick-peas triple in volume after soaking and cooking, so you may need to reduce the amount of onions or tomatoes depending on the size of your pressure cooker. Make sure you do not fill the cooker more than half full.

2 1/2 cups water
1 1/2 cups dried chick-peas, soaked and drained
5 1/2 cups chicken broth
1 1/2 cups canned Italian plum tomatoes, drained and chopped
1 cup lentils
1 cup fresh Italian parsley, stemmed and chopped
1 cup cilantro, stemmed and chopped
1/2 cup brown rice
2 medium yellow onions, finely chopped
1 tablespoon tomato paste
1 teaspoon coarse-ground black pepper
1/2 teaspoon crumbled saffron threads
Salt and pepper to taste

Add chick-peas and water to cooker, bring to high pressure, and cook for 10 minutes. Reduce pressure quickly under cold water, add remaining ingredients, and bring to high pressure again. Cook for 30 more minutes. Let pressure fall on its own. Serve hot. This dish can be stored in the refrigerator for up to 3 days.

Serves 8

Cioppino

This hearty fish chowder goes well with crusty Italian bread. The flavorful twist in this recipe is in adding half of the fish to the tomato broth at the start of cooking and the remainder just before serving.

3 tablespoons minced garlic
2 pounds skinned boneless fish
1 can (28 ounces) chopped peeled tomatoes, drained
1 ½ cups dry white wine
3 teaspoons crumbled dried oregano, or 2 teaspoons fresh, chopped
1 teaspoon honey
¼ teaspoon cayenne pepper
2 bay leaves
½ teaspoon freshly ground pepper
10 to 12 littleneck or cherrystone clams, in the shell
½ cup chopped Italian parsley, for garnish

Coat cooker with nonstick spray and brown garlic. Add half the fish and the rest of the ingredients, except clams. Bring to high pressure on medium heat and cook for 3 minutes. Reduce pressure under cold water, remove lid, add clams and fish, and cook under pressure for 2 more minutes. Reduce pressure quickly under cold water. Remove bay leaves, add parsley, and serve.

Serves 4

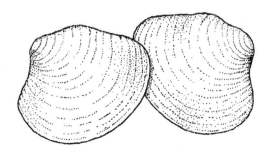

Savory Lentil Stew

Cooking beans with molasses increases the calcium absorption.

4 1/2 cups nonfat chicken broth
2 cups brown lentils, washed and drained
1 tablespoon molasses
2 teaspoons dried thyme
1 bay leaf
1/4 teaspoon salt
1/4 teaspoon ground pepper
2 strips orange peel, 1/2-inch wide
2 yellow onions, chopped
2 tablespoons minced garlic
6 boneless skinless chicken thighs
4 stalks celery, chopped
3 carrots, chopped
1 tablespoon olive oil
1 cup dry white wine
Small bunch parsley, chopped

Add to pressure cooker along with chicken broth, lentils, molasses, thyme, bay leaf, salt, pepper, and orange peel. Cook under pressure for 15 minutes. In separate pan, brown onions, garlic, chicken thighs, celery, and carrots in olive oil. Add wine and cook 2 to 3 minutes, or until wine is slightly reduced. When lentils are finished remove bay leaf, top with chicken mixture, sprinkle with parsley, and serve.

Serves 6

Potato, Lentil, and Wild Mushroom Stew

Shiitake mushrooms are available fresh or dried. They are particularly well suited for use in soups and stews since their garlic-pine aroma and stronger flavor do not get lost in the soup pot. Recent studies indicate that shiitake mushrooms appear to have a strong medicinal effect and may even have anti-cancer properties. Nutritionally, shiitake mushrooms are also a good source of fiber and the B vitamins niacin, thiamin, and riboflavin. Porcini mushrooms are wild mushrooms that also work well in this soup. They are all the rage in gourmet cooking and can be purchased fresh or dried in packages.

3/4 ounce dried shiitake mushrooms
6 cups lowfat beef broth
3/4 cup sliced shallots
1 1/2 pounds russet potatoes, chopped
1/2 pound fully cooked reduced-fat sausage (such as kielbasa),
    sliced
1 cup lentils, rinsed and drained (no need to soak or precook)
1 teaspoon dried thyme

Add mushrooms to beef broth and let soak while preparing other ingredients. Coat pan with nonstick spray and brown shallots. Add all ingredients, including mushrooms and broth, bring to high pressure on medium heat, and cook for 20 minutes.

Serves 8

Saffron Seafood Stew

Saffron threads are the stamens of flowers and the yellow color they impart comes from the pollen.

2 large onions, diced
2 teaspoons minced garlic
2 cups water
1 can (28 ounces) chopped tomatoes, drained, liquid reserved
3 medium potatoes, peeled and diced
1 small butternut squash, peeled, seeded, and cut into cubes
1 strip orange zest, 1 × 3-inch
1 bay leaf
$1/2$ teaspoon saffron threads dissolved in $1/4$ cup boiling water
$1/2$ teaspoon ground fennel seed
Pinch ground cloves
1 $1/2$ pounds codfish steak, cut into 1-inch pieces
1 tablespoon fresh or frozen lemon juice
Salt and pepper to taste
$1/4$ cup minced parsley

Coat cooker with nonstick spray and cook onions and garlic until soft but not brown. Add water, vegetables, orange zest, bay leaf, saffron, fennel seed, and cloves. Bring to high pressure and cook for 6 minutes. Reduce pressure quickly under cold water and add fish. Again bring to high pressure and cook for 1 $1/2$ minutes. Reduce pressure under cold water, season with lemon juice, salt, and pepper. Garnish with parsley.

Serves 4

CHAPTER 9

Vegetables

Vegetables are the edible roots and tubers, stems, leaves, fruits, and flow-
ers of plants. They include: root and tuber vegetables such as potatoes,
yams, rutabagas, turnips, carrots, and parsnips; stem vegetables such as
asparagus, celery, onions, and leeks; leaf vegetables such as spinach,
kale, collards, cabbage, and chard; fruit vegetables such as tomatoes,
eggplant, peppers, green peas, beans, and corn; and flower vegetables
such as artichokes, broccoli, and cauliflower. Vegetables are rich sources
of vitamins, minerals, and cancer-preventive phytochemicals.

Numerous health organizations and government agencies recommend eating a minimum of 5 servings of fruits and vegetables
each day. Pressure-cooking vegetables makes that goal easier to
reach. Root and tuber vegetables that are heavy, hard, and full of
starch are perfect for the pressure cooker. They benefit from the
high temperature and moist heat. However, even delicate leafy
greens such as kale and spinach can benefit by being prepared in
the pressure cooker. The pressure cooker seals in their flavor and
color and reduces cooking odors.

A general rule of thumb is, root vegetables take longer to
cook than stem, leaf, or flower vegetables. Since cooking time is
determined by size, you can decrease the time by cutting vegetables into small pieces. Cooking time is also determined by the
age of the vegetable. Mature vegetables take longer to cook than
tender baby vegetables.

Since delicate leaf and stem vegetables cook so quickly, ac-
curate timing is extremely important. A minute too long and
steamed spinach becomes spinach mush. Always use a timer
when cooking vegetables (a digital timer is best) and don't leave

the kitchen. Reduce pressure quickly for stem and leaf vegetables to prevent additional cooking.

Tips for Cooking Vegetables

- Check your pressure cooker's instruction manual for minimum amounts of cooking liquid.
- If you like your vegetables soft, or if you are going to puree them, cook them longer.
- Always quick-cool under cold water.
- A "0" cooking time means to cook vegetable just until high pressure is reached (when the regulator begins to rock or hiss), cool quickly under cold water, and remove lid immediately.
- Increase cooking time slightly when using a casserole dish or bowl to hold vegetables.
- Delicate vegetables should be cooked using the rack or bowl.
- Make sure no pieces of vegetables touch the sides of cooker. They will absorb heat from the walls of the cooker and burn or overcook where they touch.
- Several different vegetables with similar cooking times may be cooked at once if the rack is used. The steam will not carry flavors.
- If you want vegetable flavors to mix, do not use the trivet. The liquid will carry and mingle the flavors.

Nutrition Tips

- If you are concerned about aluminum, use a stainless steel or glass ovenproof bowl inside the cooker.
- If you don't have time to shop frequently for fresh vegetables, keep your freezer stocked with frozen vegies.
- Mix your vegetables for variety.

Frozen Vegetable Timetable

Add 3 to 5 minutes when cooking vegetables in a separate container.

VEGETABLE	COOKING TIME AT HIGH PRESSURE
Asparagus	2 minutes
Beans, green or wax	1 to 3 minutes
Broccoli	2 to 3 minutes
Brussels sprouts	2 to 2 1/2 minutes
Cauliflower	1 to 2 minutes
Corn on the cob	2 minutes
Corn, kernels	1 minute
Lima beans	2 to 4 minutes
Mixed vegetables	2 minutes
Peas	1 minute
Spinach	1 minute

Fresh Vegetable Timetable

- *Times are approximate.*
- *Add 3 to 5 minutes when cooking vegetables in a separate container.*
- *Add 1 to 4 minutes when steaming vegetables on the trivet.*
- *Cook vegetables for a shorter time if you like them crisper or longer if you like them well done.*

VEGETABLE	SIZE	COOKING TIME AT HIGH PRESSURE
Artichoke, globe Wash, trim tops, and score hearts. Tie ends to hold shape.	Whole	9 to 11 minutes
Asparagus Wash and trim tough ends and scales. Tips cook faster than stem pieces.	Spears or 1-inch pieces	0 to 2 1/2 minutes
Beans, green or wax Wash, remove strings, trim ends. Pieces cook faster than whole beans.	Whole or cut	1 to 3 minutes

Fresh Vegetable Timetable, continued

VEGETABLE	SIZE	COOKING TIME AT HIGH PRESSURE
Beans, fresh lima Shell and wash	Whole	3/4 to 1 minute
Beets Cut off tops and wash. Remove skin before serving.	Small, whole Large, whole	11 to 13 minutes 15 to 18 minutes
Broccoli Wash, trim outer leaves, and score large stems.	Spears	2 to 4 minutes
Brussels sprouts Wash and trim stems if necessary.	Whole	5 minutes
Cabbage (green or red) Wash. Trim damaged leaves.	Shredded Wedges	2 to 3 minutes 5 to 8 minutes
Carrots Remove tops and wash.	Whole Slices	3 to 5 minutes 2 minutes
Cauliflower Cut off stem, wash, break into florets and trim any discoloration.	Whole Florets	6 to 8 minutes 2 to 3 minutes
Celery Wash and remove tough fibers.	Slices	3 to 5 minutes
Collards and Kale Wash thoroughly and remove tough veins. Cut into slices.	2-inch pieces	4 to 6 minutes
Corn Remove husk and silk and wash. Cook cobs on rack.	Kernels On the cob	3 minutes 4 to 5 minutes

VEGETABLE	SIZE	COOKING TIME AT HIGH PRESSURE
Eggplant Wash and cut into cubes. Cook immediately to prevent discoloration.	1-inch cubes	3 minutes
Greens (beet greens, collards, kale, spinach, Swiss chard, turnip greens)	Whole leaves	1 to 4 minutes
Kohlrabi Wash, peel, and cut into pieces.	1-inch cubes	3 to 4 minutes
Onions Wash and peel.	Whole Sliced	6 to 9 minutes 3 minutes
Parsnips Peel and wash. Cook slices on rack.	Halves 1/2-inch slices	6 to 8 minutes 1 to 2 minutes
Peas Shell and wash.	Whole	0 to 2 minutes
Potatoes Scrub and slice if desired. Cook on rack.	Whole, medium 1/2-inch slices Halves	12 to 15 minutes 2 to 3 minutes 8 to 10 minutes
Potatoes, sweet and Yams Scrub and cut in half if desired.	Whole, medium Halves	10 to 11 minutes 8 to 10 minutes
Pumpkins Cut in large pieces, remove seeds and pulp. Wash.	Wedges	8 to 10 minutes
Rutabagas and Turnips Wash, peel, and cut into cubes or slices.	1/2-inch slices	3 to 5 minutes

Fresh Vegetable Timetable, continued

VEGETABLE	SIZE	COOKING TIME AT HIGH PRESSURE
Squash, acorn Wash, cut in half and remove seeds. Cook on rack.	Halves	6 to 7 minutes
Squash, hubbard Wash and cut into pieces. Cook on rack.	1-inch cubes	8 to 10 minutes
Squash, summer and Zucchini Wash, cut in pieces or slices. Cook on rack.	1-inch slices	2 to 3 minutes
Sweet peppers Wash, remove seeds, and core.	Whole	1 to 3 minutes
Tomatoes Wash and cut into pieces if desired.	Whole	2 to 3 minutes

Artichokes in Garlic Sauce

This is an easy-to-make, fun-to-eat starter.

1 to 2 cups water
3 small artichokes

Sauce
3 tablespoons crushed garlic
3 tablespoons butter

Place artichokes in pressure cooker, bring to high pressure immediately, and cook for 6 minutes. Reduce pressure immediately under cold water, open, and set artichokes in serving dishes. Use open pressure cooker to melt butter and brown garlic. Serve garlic butter as a dip for the artichoke leaves and to coat the heart.

Serves 3

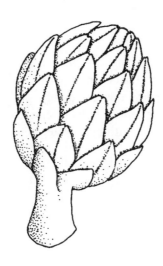

Vegetable Casserole

A perfect way to increase your family's consumption of vegetables, this casserole should be composed with color in mind as well as taste and texture. Mix green, yellow, red, white, and orange vegetables and this recipe will look as good as it tastes. To add a crowning touch, top with one of the sauces that follow.

1 to 2 cups water
1/2 cup fresh broccoli or cauliflower florets
1/2 cup sliced carrots or zucchini
1/2 cup large frozen peas
1/2 cup onions (boiler, yellow, or green), sliced
1/4 cup sliced red or green bell pepper
1/4 teaspoon pepper
1/2 to 1 teaspoon mixed herbs
2 tablespoons chopped fresh parsley

Equipment
Trivet
Ovenproof casserole dish, well-oiled
Cover for dish

Pour the recommended amount of water into your pressure cooker and place trivet inside. In casserole dish, combine all ingredients except parsley, cover securely, and place on top of trivet. Bring to high pressure quickly and cook for 2 minutes. Quickly reduce pressure with cold water, remove casserole, and sprinkle with parsley.

Serves 4

Variations

Frozen Vegie Casserole

Substitute: frozen corn for broccoli or cauliflower florets

Substitute: frozen pearl onions for sliced onions

Substitute: frozen lima beans for zucchini

Substitute: frozen French-style green beans for carrots

Pesto Zucchini and Peppers

Substitute: 1 cup zucchini, 1/2 cup thinly sliced carrots, 1/2 cup thickly sliced red bell peppers, 1/2 cup thick yellow peppers for vegetables

Omit: dried herbs

Add: 1 can (15 ounces) chopped tomatoes with juice

Add: 1 tablespoon pesto

Sauces for Vegetables

To turn your hot cooked vegetables into a meal, serve over a bed of pasta, rice, or whole wheat couscous and crown with one of these sauces.

Salmon Sauce

6 to 8 ounces canned salmon (or drained water-packed tuna)
Dash Tabasco sauce
1 1/2 tablespoons lemon juice
1 cup yogurt or mayonnaise

Hot Crab Sauce

1 cup cooked or canned crab
8 ounces cream cheese, softened
1/4 cup milk
1 teaspoon horseradish
1 tablespoon minced onion
1 tablespoon lemon juice

Combine ingredients and heat gently. If sauce is too thick, add 1 teaspoon more milk. This recipe also works well using drained canned tuna or salmon.

Creamy Dill Sauce

2 tablespoons chopped green onions
1 cup milk
1 tablespoon arrowroot mixed with 2 tablespoons cold milk
1/4 teaspoon dried dill
Salt and pepper to taste

Combine ingredients in pan and mix well. Cook on medium heat until sauce starts to thicken. Serve warm over cooked vegetables.

Hot Curry Sauce

1 cup yogurt (or 3/4 cup yogurt plus 1/4 cup mayonnaise)
1/2 teaspoon curry powder
1/2 teaspoon prepared mustard

Combine ingredients in small saucepan. Heat to boiling and serve warm over vegetables.

Cheese Sauce

1/2 cup milk
1/2 cup yogurt
1 tablespoon cornstarch mixed with 2 tablespoons of the milk
Pinch dry mustard
Salt and pepper to taste
1/4 cup grated or shredded

In a saucepan combine all ingredients except cheese. Heat until thickened. Stir in cheese and serve immediately over vegetables.

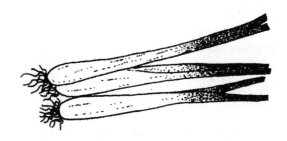

Asparagus with Lemon-Dill Sauce

Asparagus that is thin and young will cook in less time than thick and mature asparagus. If you like your asparagus crisp, cook it for the minimal length of time. For a more béarnaise-like sauce, substitute 1/8 teaspoon dried chervil plus 1/8 teaspoon dried tarragon for the dill.

1/2 to 1 cup water
1 1/2 pounds asparagus stalks

Equipment
Trivet

Pour the recommended amount of water into your pressure cooker and place trivet inside. Lay asparagus on trivet, bring to high pressure, and cook for 0 to 2 minutes. Reduce pressure quickly under cold water and serve with sauce that follows.

Serves 4

Sauce
1 1/2 teaspoons cornstarch dissolved in 1/4 cup cold water
1 tablespoon butter
1/4 teaspoon grated lemon peel
1 1/2 teaspoons lemon juice
1 1/2 teaspoons minced onion
1/4 teaspoon dried dill
1/4 cup yogurt

Combine all ingredients, except yogurt, in saucepan and mix until thickened. Stir in yogurt and serve over asparagus or other vegetables.

Serves 4

Glazed Carrots and Shallots

This recipe lends itself well to many root vegetables such as turnips, parsnips, and rutabagas, so use what you have available. If you like garlic and onions, you will love the shallots in this recipe. Add up to 1 full cup of sliced shallots for a real delicacy.

1 pound carrots, peeled and thinly sliced (about 1/4-inch thick)
1/2 cup vegetable broth
1/4 cup shallots, minced
3 tablespoons red wine vinegar
1 tablespoon sugar
1/4 cup Italian parsley, stemmed and chopped

Add carrots, broth, and shallots and cook under pressure for 5 to 7 minutes, depending on size of carrots. When finished, add vinegar and sugar, glazing carrots completely. Add parsley and serve.

Serves 6

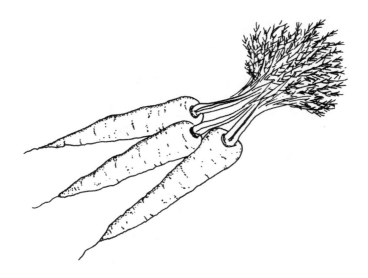

Ginger-Tomato Spaghetti Sauce

Serve over spaghetti squash, pasta, or cooked grains.

3 shallots, chopped
1 tablespoon minced garlic
1 tablespoon minced ginger
1 large can (28 ounces) crushed tomatoes with juice
2 cups vegetable broth
1 tablespoon soy sauce

Coat cooker with nonstick spray and cook shallots and garlic for 1 minute. Add remaining ingredients, bring to high pressure, and cook for 20 minutes.

Serves 4

Mashed Sweet Potatoes with Balsamic Vinegar

1 to 2 cups water (depending on size of machine)
5 large sweet potatoes, scrubbed, peeled, and cut into 1-inch
   slices
1 cup milk
2 teaspoons balsamic vinegar
1 teaspoon ground cinnamon
1 teaspoon freshly grated nutmeg

Equipment
Trivet, well-oiled

Pour water into pressure cooker, add trivet, and lay sweet potatoes on top. Bring to high pressure quickly and cook for 8 minutes. Reduce pressure quickly under cold water. Remove potatoes, mash, and beat in milk, vinegar, cinnamon, and nutmeg.

Serves 4

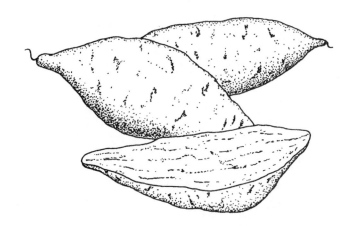

Green Beans with Tomatoes and Sesame Seeds

Sesame seeds are nice with the beans but other nuts are also delicious. Try sliced almonds or chopped walnuts.

2 tablespoons minced garlic
1 medium yellow onion, finely chopped
1 pound green beans, topped and tailed
1 can (14.4 ounces) Italian plum tomatoes, drained and chopped
1/2 cup vegetable broth
1 teaspoon honey
Salt to taste
1 tablespoon fresh or frozen lemon juice
2 tablespoons sesame seeds

Coat cooker with nonstick spray and brown garlic and onion. Add remaining ingredients except lemon juice and sesame seeds, bring to high pressure, and cook for 3 minutes. Reduce pressure quickly under cold water, add lemon juice and sesame seeds, and serve.

Serves 6

Hot Potato Salad

Serve this salad cold or hot. It's a good dish for summer picnics and potlucks.

1 to 2 cups water
3 cups small red potatoes, cut in half
1/4 cup chopped green onions
Salt to taste
2 tablespoons balsamic vinegar
1/4 cup sour cream
2 hard-boiled eggs, sliced
1 teaspoon paprika

Equipment
Trivet
Ovenproof casserole dish, well-oiled
Cover for dish

Pour water into pressure cooker and put trivet in place. Combine potatoes, onions, and salt (if any) in dish and sprinkle with vinegar. Bring to high pressure quickly and cook for 10 to 12 minutes. Reduce pressure quickly, remove dish, and stir in sour cream and egg slices. Sprinkle with paprika and serve warm or cold.

Serves 6

Confetti Corn

A good looking and great tasting side dish.

1 to 2 cups water
1 cup frozen corn
½ cup frozen peas
½ cup chopped red bell pepper
¼ cup frozen pearl onions
1 teaspoon mixed herbs

Equipment
Trivet
Ovenproof casserole dish, well-oiled
Cover for dish

Pour the recommended amount of water into your pressure cooker and place trivet inside. In casserole dish, combine all ingredients, cover securely, and place on top of trivet. Bring to high pressure quickly, cook for 4 to 6 minutes, and reduce pressure quickly under cold water.

Serves 4

CHAPTER 10

Fruit

Fruit is the fleshy tissues that surround some seeds. Dried fruit has had most of the water removed to increase storage life. Fruits are a good source of natural sugar and the antioxidant vitamins and dried fruits are a good source of trace minerals.

*F*ruit is the original dessert and is always the best choice for those with a sweet tooth. Fresh fruit assumes a new identity when steamed or poached in the pressure cooker. A simple pear can be transformed into elegant dessert for company. Dried fruit is renewed and plumped full of new flavors. Dried pressure-cooked fruit can be used as a topping, a sweet treat, or as an addition to breads, cakes, and other recipes.

Since fresh fruit cooks very quickly, a timer is a must. A minute may mean the difference between a poached apple and applesauce.

Tips for Cooking Fresh Fruit

- If you want to sweeten cooking fruit, add sugar, honey, or molasses after cooking. Thick sweeteners can stick to the bottom of the pan and burn. Syrups can also delay the absorption of water into dried fruit and prolong cooking time.

- Make sure that the fruit does not touch the sides of the cooker. This can cause fruit to burn.

Tips for Cooking Dried Fruit

- Fruit can be rehydrated in water, wine, juices, and liquors and flavored with extracts such as rum, vanilla, and almond.
- Seasonings such as allspice, whole cloves, coriander, cinnamon, ginger, lavender, mint, and nutmeg work well with stewed fruit.
- The natural sweetness of dried fruit does not need the addition of sweeteners. However, you can add small amounts of brown or white sugar, date sugar, honey, molasses, maple syrup, fruit concentrate, or rice syrup.
- Citrus flavors such as lime and lemon juice and citrus peel and zest add high notes to stewed fruit.
- For all dried fruit, reduce pressure instantly by quick-cooling under the faucet.
- Dried fruit can be presoaked. Liquors and juices make good presoaking liquids.
- Do not fill cooker more than half full. Dried fruit will swell with cooking and could block the vent pipe.
- Add a few small pieces of fresh fruit such as grapes, cherries, diced apples or pears, bananas, pineapple chunks, or citrus fruit sections to dishes made with dried fruit.

Fresh Fruit Timetable

Since fresh fruit cooks so fast, a timer is a necessity. These times are approximate. How fast fresh fruit cooks depends upon the degree of ripeness. Very ripe fruit will cook faster than underripe fruit.

FRESH FRUIT	COOKING TIME AT HIGH PRESSURE
Apples*	4 to 6 minutes
Apricots*	5 to 7 minutes
Bananas*	6 to 7 minutes
Berries*	4 to 6 minutes
Cherries*	5 to 6 minutes
Cranberries*	4 to 6 minutes
Oranges**	2 minutes
Peach halves*	3 minutes
Pears*	6 to 8 minutes
Pineapple**	6 to 8 minutes
Plum halves*	4 to 6 minutes

* Time given is for cooking in a separate cooking dish.
** Time given is for poaching on trivet. For cooking in separate dish, add 4 to 5 minutes.

Dried Fruit Timetable

These times are approximate. How fast dried fruit cooks depends upon the degree of dehydration. If fruit is very dehydrated and is not pliable, presoak for 30 to 60 minutes. Remember, do not fill the cooker over 1/2 full.

DRIED FRUIT	COOKING TIME AT HIGH PRESSURE
Apple rings	6 minutes
Apricots	3 minutes
Cranberries	5 minutes
Dates	10 minutes

Dried Fruit Timetable, continued

DRIED FRUIT	COOKING TIME AT HIGH PRESSURE
Figs*	10 minutes
Mixed fruit	10 minutes
Peaches	4 to 5 minutes
Pears	8 to 10 minutes
Prunes	5 to 6 minutes
Raisins	5 minutes

* Must be presoaked

Date-stuffed Apples

A perfect dish for cold winter nights. Be careful not to overcook the apples or they will turn to sauce.

4 cooking apples
1 cup chopped dates
1/4 teaspoon cinnamon
4 tablespoons honey

Equipment
4 small custard cups
Cover for dish: glass cover, wax paper, foil
Trivet

Core each apple and place in glass cups. Mix chopped dates with cinnamon and stuff each apple with the mixture. Place on trivet and cook 4 to 6 minutes on high pressure. Reduce pressure quickly. Drizzle 1 tablespoon of honey over each apple before serving.

Serves 4

Poached Company Fruit

Fruit poaches quickly and easily in the pressure cooker. Poached fresh fruit is a refreshing and healthful dessert. It is the perfect dish to end the meal or begin the day. Poached fruit can be dressed up or down depending on the occasion. Following is a simple recipe that looks as great as it tastes. The brown skin of the pears pulls slightly apart during cooking, giving a cracked appearance.

4 Comice pears, cored from the bottom up with stem left intact
1 cup dry red wine
2 whole cloves
1/4 teaspoon cinnamon
4 tablespoons good-quality chocolate pieces, melted

Add wine, cloves, and cinnamon to your pressure cooker and arrange pears so that they do not touch the sides of the cooker. Carefully bring to high pressure on medium heat. If you bring up the pressure too quickly, wine can spurt out the through the vent and may catch fire. Cook for 8 minutes then reduce pressure quickly under cold water. Spoon wine into bottom of dessert or custard dish, place one pear in each dish, and drizzle one tablespoon of chocolate over the top of each pear. Serve while still warm.

Serves 4

Variations

Juice-poached Pears

Substitute: uncored pears for cored pears

Substitute: 1 cup apple or pineapple juice for wine, spices, and honey

Substitute: molasses for chocolate; place each pear in a small custard dish and drizzle with molasses. Serve warm or chilled.

Poached Apples

Substitute: apples for the pears

Substitute: water for wine

Substitute: honey for chocolate

Omit: cloves and cinnamon

Add: dust honey-coated pears with allspice

Stewed Dried Fruit

Dried fruits are concentrated sources of sugar and rarely need additional sweetening. Before adding sugar to the recipes that follow, try making them without any sweetener. You will find that the method of pressure-release affects the texture of cooked dried fruit. Experiment to find your personal preference.

Mixed Fruit Compote

This is a very sweet compote which can be used as a topping for yogurt, ice cream, pancakes, waffles, or cereal. Or serve it topped with a dollop of yogurt, custard, or vanilla pudding.

1 cup mixed dried fruit (apples, apricots, pears, prunes)
2 cups water
1 cinnamon stick
1/4 teaspoon allspice
1 tablespoon honey
1 1/2 slices lemon with peel
1 thin slice ginger root

Combine all ingredients in your pressure cooker, bring to high pressure, and cook for 3 minutes. Reduce pressure and serve. Store in refrigerator for up to 1 week.

Serves 4

Variations

Spicy Ginger Compote

Add: 1 teaspoon minced ginger root

Add: 1 cinnamon stick

Add: 2 cloves

Add: 1 teaspoon citrus zest

Add: 2 teaspoons lemon or lime juice

Raisin Topping

Substitute: 1/2 cup raisins, 1/2 cup dried cranberries, 1/2 cup dried blueberries or cherries, and 1/2 cup sultanas for the mixed fruit

Substitute: apple juice for water
Add: 2 tablespoons rum or 1 teaspoon rum extract

Add: 4 whole coriander seeds

Omit: ginger slice

Release pressure under cold water and simmer on low heat to reduce and thicken topping. Use warm or chilled. This makes a wonderful topping for ice cream, ice milk, or frozen yogurt.

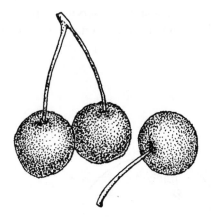

Baked Oranges

An unusual dessert that is quick and easy to make. Grapefruit also works well in this recipe.

4 large oranges
1/2 cup honey
1/4 teaspoon allspice
2 tablespoons rum
1/2 cup water

Poach unpeeled oranges in 3 cups of water, bring to high pressure, and cook for 3 minutes on high pressure. Reduce pressure quickly, drain, and remove peels. Replace oranges in cooker, add honey, allspice, rum, and water, and cook for 2 minutes at high pressure. Remove oranges to serving cups and continue cooking liquid until it thickens. Pour syrup over oranges and serve warm or chilled.

Serves 4

Brown Sugar Bananas

This is a warm, soothing dish for the stomach, a perfect comfort food.

4 large ripe bananas, peeled
2 tablespoons brown sugar
1/8 teaspoon nutmeg
1 cup water

Equipment
Ovenproof oval casserole dish
Cover for dish: glass, wax paper, foil
Trivet

Place bananas into dish, sprinkle with brown sugar and nutmeg, and cover securely. Pour water into bottom of cooker, put trivet into cooker, and place casserole dish on top of trivet. Bring to high pressure and cook for 6 to 7 minutes. Reduce pressure and serve warm.

Serves 4

CHAPTER 11

Legumes

Beans or legumes belong to the pea family. The dried edible seeds of these plants include beans, peas, and lentils. Legumes are very high in protein, complex carbohydrates, and soluble fiber, as well as good amounts of iron and calcium.

*L*egumes have often been called "the poor man's meat" because of their excellent protein content and satisfying texture. They are a staple in the diet of many nationalities. Beans and peas come in a wide variety of colors, sizes, textures, and tastes. They are easily prepared and can be dressed up or dressed down, depending on the circumstance. You can serve beans as a main course with pasta or grains, in a soup or stew, mashed for a dip or filling, as a cold salad, or as a dip for vegetables.

Dried beans should be rehydrated before they are cooked. There are two methods for doing this.

1. Soak overnight

Wash beans and pick through. Put 3 cups of water to every cup of beans in a bowl, add 2 teaspoons of salt, and let sit overnight. Drain well and proceed with recipe.

2. Quick-soak

Wash beans and pick through. Place in pressure cooker with 3 cups of water for every cup of beans, add 2 teaspoons of salt, bring beans and liquid to high pressure, and cook for 5 minutes. Remove from heat and let pressure fall on its own. Drain well and proceed with recipe.

Beans are notorious for causing gas, due to the presence of oligosaccharides. Human digestive enzymes cannot completely break down this compound. Much of it passes unchanged into the large intestine where bacteria eat it and produce gas as a byproduct.

When beans soak, oligosaccharides are lost to the water. This is why most methods of soaking beans call for presoaking and discarding the water. Another good method of preventing gas is to add a product called Beano to the first tablespoon of beans eaten. This product supplies the enzyme necessary to digest the oligosaccharides. Look for it in your health food store or supermarket.

Tips for Cooking Legumes

- Store dried beans in tightly covered containers in a cool dry place, and they will keep for months. Do not store in refrigerator. Adding a couple of bay leaves to each container is said to discourage insects and other unwanted creatures.
- Dried beans double in volume and weight after soaking and cooking. Rule of Thumb: 1 cup (8 ounces) dried beans equals 2 to 2 1/2 cups (1 to 1 1/4 pounds) soaked and cooked.
- Never fill cooker more than half full. The beans will expand and could plug the vent.
- Add a tablespoon of cooking oil to help prevent loose bean skins from clogging the pressure vent. This is especially important with split peas and lentils.
- Dried black-eyed peas, lentils, and split peas do not need to be presoaked. Simply rinse and pick over thoroughly to remove any pebbles, dust, and other debris.
- When buying canned beans, read labels. Look for organic and just beans in water. Avoid those that list preservatives, additives, salt, and sugar.

- Avoid adding salt to cooking water. Salt toughens the skins and prevents water from being absorbed. But do add salt to the soaking water. It will help the beans prepare for cooking.
- Soaked beans (both overnight and quick-soaked) can be stored in the freezer for up to 2 months.

Nutrition Tips

- Legumes are the perfect diet food. They are low in fat and calories and high in complex carbohydrates and insoluble fiber.
- The soluble fiber in legumes can reduce high cholesterol levels and aid in the prevention of colon cancer.
- Legumes keep blood sugar levels even, important for those who have diabetes or hypoglycemia.
- If you are worried about the aluminum content of your cooker, place a stainless steel bowl on top of the trivet. Add liquid to the cooker first then fit the stainless steel bowl into the cooker. Add beans and an equal amount of water to bowl. Cover and cook as directed.

Legumes Timetable

Before pressure-cooking, place beans (except lentils and split peas) in the cooker with 2 cups of water for every 1 cup of dried beans and 2 teaspoons of salt. Bring water and beans to high pressure for 5 minutes, remove from heat, and let pressure fall on its own. Drain off salted water and cook in pressure cooker according to table. If you prefer to soak beans overnight, add 3 to 4 minutes to the cooking times.

LEGUME	COOKING TIME AT HIGH PRESSURE *
Adzuki beans	2 to 3 minutes
Black-eyed peas	10 minutes
Black beans	5 to 8 minutes

LEGUME	COOKING TIME AT HIGH PRESSURE *
Cannellini beans	5 to 8 minutes
Chick-peas (Garbanzo beans)	10 to 13 minutes
Cranberry	5 to 9 minutes
Great Northerns	4 to 9 minutes
Kidney beans	4 to 8 minutes
Lentils*	9 to 12 minutes
Lima beans	1 to 3 minutes
Navy beans	3 to 5 minutes
Pintos, pink or white	1 to 3 minutes
Small white	10 minutes
Soybeans	35 minutes
Split peas*	6 to 10 minutes
Whole peas	4 to 6 minutes

*Cooking times are approximate. Actual cooking time varies according to type of pressure cooker, growing conditions, and the age of the beans.

Refried Black Beans

A tasty alternative to the traditional refried pinto beans.

2 yellow onions, chopped
1 tablespoon minced garlic
2 cups quick-soaked black beans, drained
2 cups chicken broth
1 teaspoon cumin
1 teaspoon chili powder

Coat cooker with nonstick spray, and brown onions. Add remaining ingredients, bring to high pressure, and cook for 10 minutes. Mash mixture with a potato masher.

Serves 4

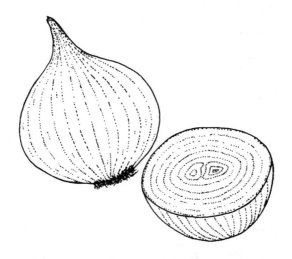

Bean Casserole

This versatile recipe can be served as a side dish or over grains.

1 yellow onion, sliced
1 red bell pepper, sliced
1 leek, sliced
1 1/2 cups water
2 cups quick-soaked cannellini beans, drained

Coat cooker with nonstick spray and brown onion, pepper, and leek. Add water and beans, bring to high pressure, and cook for 8 minutes. Let pressure fall on its own.

Serves 4

Variations

Tomatoes and Beans

Add: 1 cup chopped tomatoes

Add: 1/2 cup Greek or black olives

Add: 1/2 cup sun-dried tomatoes, chopped

Add: Feta cheese sprinkled on top for garnish

Beans and Greens

Substitute: 2 cups bok choy for leeks

Add: 1 tablespoon fresh thyme, or 1/2 tablespoon dried

Spicy Beans

Add: 1 small green chili pepper, chopped

Add: 1 teaspoon red chili flakes

Substitute: Red kidney beans for cannellini beans; increase cooking time to 10 minutes.

Mediterranean Black Beans

This dish is spicy. If your taste buds are sensitive, reduce the garlic and the pepper sauce.

1 cup onions, chopped
3 tablespoons minced garlic (about 18 cloves)
2 cups chicken or vegetable broth
1 1/2 cups quick-soaked black beans, drained
1 large red bell pepper, seeded and chopped
1 large green bell pepper, seeded and chopped
1/2 cup sun-dried tomatoes, chopped
2 tablespoons dried oregano
1 tablespoon garlic chili pepper sauce
1 bay leaf
3 teaspoons red wine vinegar
1/2 cup cilantro, chopped

Coat cooker with nonstick spray, brown onions and garlic, and add the remaining ingredients except vinegar and cilantro. Bring cooker to high pressure and cook for 15 minutes. Reduce pressure, stir in vinegar, and top with cilantro.

Serves 4

Refried Beans

Pinto beans are traditionally used for refried beans but black beans are delicious also. Spice up or down as much as you like.

2 cups quick-soaked pinto beans, drained
2 whole garlic cloves, peeled
1 large onion, quartered
4 cups water
1 teaspoon chili powder
1 teaspoon cumin
Olive oil (optional)

Add beans, garlic, onion, and water to cooker, bring to high pressure, and cook for 15 minutes. Drain well and mash with potato masher. Add chili powder, cumin, and olive oil if desired and mix well. Serve with sautéed onions or salsa. Adding a little more olive oil to the beans after cooking will give beans a creamier texture.

Serves 4

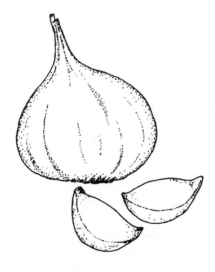

Lentil Hummus

If you are a garlic lover, feel free to add as much minced garlic as you can handle. It is traditional to have generous amounts of olive oil and lemon juice floating on top of the hummus when served but if calories are a concern you can omit the oil. Hummus can be served with tortilla wedges or thin sliced carrots for dipping.

1 medium yellow onion, minced
1 tablespoon minced garlic
1 cup lentils, red, yellow, or green, rinsed and drained
2 1/2 cups chicken broth
1 teaspoon allspice
Juice of 1 lemon
Olive oil (optional)

Brown onions and garlic in nonstick spray then add lentils, broth, and allspice, bring to high pressure on medium, and cook for 15 minutes. Reduce pressure under cold water, open lid, and stir. Let hummus sit for 5 to 10 minutes to release steam and thicken. Pour into serving dish and sprinkle with lemon juice and olive oil.

Serves 4

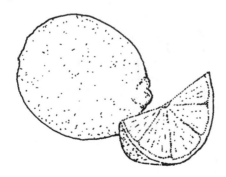

Spicy Vegetable Dahl

Dried split peas do not need to be presoaked. Simply rinse and pick over thoroughly.

1 yellow onion, chopped
1 tablespoon minced garlic
4 cups vegetable broth
1 can (28 ounces) plum tomatoes
1 cup split peas, rinsed and drained
1 fennel bulb, chopped
2 tablespoons minced ginger
1 tablespoon cumin
1 teaspoon turmeric
1/4 teaspoon ground clove powder

Coat cooker with nonstick spray, brown onions and garlic, and add the rest of the ingredients. Bring to high pressure on medium heat, and cook for 10 minutes. Let pressure fall on its own.

Serves 4

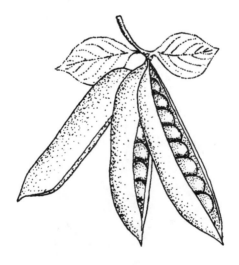

Ham and Bean Hash

Canned vegetables can also replace the fresh in this recipe if time is a concern. Two cups of vegetable equals about one 14 1/2 ounce can.

1 large onion, chopped
2 cups quick-soaked kidney beans, drained
2 cups chopped tomatoes
2 cups diced new potatoes
2 cups frozen corn
8 ounces cooked ham, sliced
2 tablespoons tomato paste
1 tablespoon Worcestershire sauce
1 tablespoon soy sauce
Tabasco sauce to taste
Salt and pepper to taste

Coat cooker with nonstick spray and add all ingredients. Bring to high pressure and cook for 15 minutes. Reduce pressure, season, and serve.

Serves 4

Chick-peas and Chicken

A wonderful pairing.

2 cups chopped chicken, white meat only
2 yellow onions, sliced
1 tablespoon chopped garlic (about 6 cloves)
2 cups quick-soaked chick-peas, drained
1 can (28 ounces) plum tomatoes with juice
1/2 cup water or broth
1 teaspoon cumin
1 teaspoon allspice
1 teaspoon turmeric powder

Coat cooker with nonstick spray, brown chicken, onions, and garlic, and add the rest of the ingredients. Bring to high pressure and cook for 10 minutes. Reduce pressure quickly and serve.

Serves 4

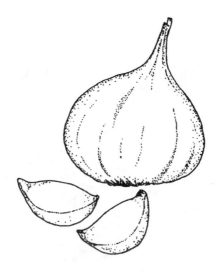

Mild Vegetarian Chili

Chili lovers will want to increase the cumin and chili powder. For more heat, add red pepper flakes. Kidney beans can be substituted for all or some of the pinto beans.

1 large onion, finely chopped
1 teaspoon minced garlic (about 2 cloves)
4 cups quick-soaked pinto beans, drained (about 2 cups dry)
1 can (32 ounces) crushed tomatoes
1 green bell pepper, chopped
1 rib celery, chopped
1 teaspoon powdered cumin
1 teaspoon chili powder

Coat cooker with nonstick spray, brown onion and garlic, and then add presoaked beans, tomatoes, green pepper, celery, cumin, and chili powder. Bring pressure to high, cook for 4 to 6 minutes, and let pressure fall on its own.

Serves 4

Bean and Chicken Enchiladas

An easy-to-make, healthful alternative to greasy fast-food enchiladas. If you want to reduce calories further, substitute lowfat cheddar cheese. This dish is also good without chicken.

1 pound ground chicken or turkey (breast meat only, no skin),
    chopped into small pieces
1 onion, chopped
2 cups quick-soaked black beans, drained
2 cups water
1 teaspoon cumin
1 teaspoon chili powder
Salt to taste
4 whole wheat tortillas
1 can (10 ounces) enchilada sauce
1/4 cup grated smoked gouda cheese
1/4 cup grated cheddar cheese
1 cup salsa
1/2 cup chopped cilantro

Equipment
Baking dish large enough to hold tortillas
Plate
Spoon

Coat pan with nonstick spray and brown ground chicken pieces and onions. Add beans, water, cumin, and chili powder to cooker, bring to high pressure, and cook for 10 minutes. Let pressure fall on its own, open, and season to taste.

Coat tortillas with enchilada sauce on both sides and then place in oiled baking dish. Spoon one quarter of the meat mixture down the center of each tortilla, fold edges to form a rectangular envelope, and turn over so that "seams" are underneath. Pour remaining enchilada sauce over folded tortillas and top each one with some of the cheese mixture. Bake at 350° for 10 minutes or until the cheese is melted. Serve with salsa and cilantro.

Serves 4

CHAPTER 12

Grains

Grains or cereals are members of the grass family and are actually tiny, separate, dry fruits. Included in this family are barley, millet, oats, rice, rye, and wheat. Technically not grains, quinoa and wild rice are sometimes referred to as "pseudograins." They are used in the kitchen as grains but belong to different botanical families. Whole grains are excellent sources of complex carbohydrates, fiber, protein, the B vitamins, and trace minerals. When it comes to grains and pseudograins, less processing means more nutrition, so always try to eat your grains in as whole a form as you can find.

No longer do you have to nurse a slow-cooking pot of grains. Pressure cooking produces breakfast and dinner grains in a fraction of the time of other methods of cooking. No longer is there any need to presoak. Pressure cooking makes all grains instant grains without any loss of flavor, texture, or nutrition.

Experiment with serving grains as a quick and nutritious alternative to potatoes or stuffing. Do not be afraid to experiment with a variety of cooking liquids. Homemade stock, canned broth, vegetable juices, and wine all add taste notes to dinner grains. Any grain can be served for breakfast. Try soaking or cooking in apple juice, orange juice and other fruit juices, soymilk, nut milks, and sweet wines.

Tips for Cooking Grains

- One cup of rice yields about 2 ½ cups of cooked grain.
- Never fill the cooker over half full. Cooking grains need room to expand.

- Grains can be cooked or steamed in the pressure cooker. To steam grains, place ovenproof dish or stainless steel bowl on top of trivet and cover loosely with a glass cover or waxed paper. Pour at least 1 1/2 cups of water in the bottom of the cooker.
- Cooking times for grains depend on the age of the grain and how dry it is, and can vary greatly.
- Short-grain brown rice takes longer to cook than long- or medium-grain.
- Always add 1 tablespoon canola oil, olive oil, or butter, to reduce foaming when cooking without a bowl.
- Let the pressure fall on its own for 5 to 10 minutes.

Nutrition Tips

- Store brown rice and other whole grains in a cool dark place and remember it has a limited storage life. The natural oils in brown rice go rancid after prolonged storage.
- Each grain has its own unique nutritional value. Try eating a variety of grains.
- Grains can be a wonderful source of protein. Just combine the grains in a meal with beans, meat, cheese, or milk (soy or dairy).
- Whole grains are also an excellent source of fiber, both soluble and insoluble. If you suffer from diabetes, high blood cholesterol, or irregularity, always cook your grains whole.

Timetable for Steaming Grains

The best way to steam grains is to place them in a heat-proof bowl. Add at least 1 1/2 cups of water to the bottom of the cooker, place the trivet inside, and place the bowl on top of the trivet, adding 4 to 4 1/2 cups water to the bowl. After cooking, drain grains. To calculate the amount of water to put into the bowl: add the number of cups of raw grain to the number of cups in the yield. This will give you a ballpark idea of how much liquid to use.

GRAIN (1 CUP)	COOKING TIME AT HIGH PRESSURE*	YIELD
Barley, unhulled	50 to 60 minutes	3 cups
Barley, pearled	17 to 20 minutes	3 1/2 cups
Millet	5 to 8 minutes	3 cups
Oats, groats	25 to 30 minutes	2 cups
Quinoa	4 to 7 minutes	2 1/2 cups
Rice, white	5 to 7 minutes	2 cups
Rice, brown, long	35 minutes	2 cups
Rice, brown, short	25 minutes	2 1/2 cups
Rye, berries	30 to 35 minutes	2 cups
Wheat, bulgur	5 minutes	2 1/2 cups
Wheat, berries	35 to 45 minutes	2 cups
Wild Rice	25 to 30 minutes	3 1/2 cups

*Allow pressure to fall on its own. Reduce pressure quickly under cold water

Rice Pilaf

Rice Pilaf is a welcome addition to any meal. Brown rice is more nutritious than white and tastes better too. Try making these recipes with long- or medium-grain brown rice and you will never return to plain old white.

1 cup long- or medium-grain brown rice
2 cups chicken broth (water, juice, or wine)
1 teaspoon dried mixed herbs

Place all ingredients in pressure cooker, bring to high pressure, and cook for 20 minutes. Quick-cool under cold water and test for doneness. If rice is still hard, add more liquid if necessary and bring back up to high pressure for another 5 minutes. When done, cover cooker and let rice sit for 5 minutes to finish cooking. Season to taste, fluff with fork, and serve.

Serves 4

Variations

Quick and Easy White Rice Pilaf

Substitute: white rice for brown (white rice is not as variable in cooking times as brown)

Add: 3 tablespoons chopped parsley

Add: 1/2 cup frozen peas and carrots

Add: 2 tablespoons chopped onion

Follow directions above but cook for only 7 minutes before testing for doneness.

Nutty Wild Rice Pilaf

Substitute: 1/2 cup wild rice for half of the brown rice

Add: 1/8 teaspoon black pepper

Add: 2 tablespoons chopped, slivered almonds

Add: 1/4 cup dried cranberries

Mushroom Pilaf

Substitute: 1/2 cup dry white wine for 1/2 cup of the water

Substitute: Italian seasoning for mixed herbs

Add: 1 cup chopped mushrooms

Add: 2 tablespoons snipped sun-dried tomatoes

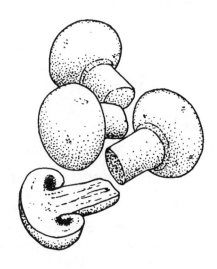

Steamed Rice

Grains can always be steamed in the pressure cooker. Find an ovenproof casserole or stainless steel bowl that fits loosely inside your cooker. Place bowl on top of trivet and add 1 1/2 cups of water to the bottom of the cooker.

1 cup long- or medium-grain brown rice
1 1/2 cups water for rice
1 1/2 cups water for cooker

Equipment
Rice bowl
Trivet

Combine water and rice in an ovenproof casserole, a metal bowl, or a boilable plastic bowl. Pour water for cooker into the bottom of the pan, put trivet into cooker, and place rice bowl on top of trivet. Bring to high pressure and cook for 30 minutes. Let pressure fall on its own and steam with cover on for a total of 15 to 30 minutes. Short-grain brown rice will take 5 to 10 minutes longer to cook than long-grain.

Serves 4

Variations

Steamed Seasoned White Rice

Substitute: Long-grain white rice for brown rice

Substitute: 1 cup nonfat chicken broth for rice water

Add: 1 teaspoon dried herbs

Follow directions for steamed rice but cook for 5 minutes on high pressure. Let pressure fall on its own, release cover but leave in place, and let rice steam for an additional 5 minutes.

Steamed Rice with Vegetables

Substitute: 1/2 cup dry white wine for 1/2 cup rice water

Substitute: 1 cup nonfat chicken broth for 1 cup rice water

Add: 1/4 cup chopped green onions

Add: 1/4 cup sliced red bell pepper

Add: 1/4 cup French-cut green beans

Add: 1/2 cup frozen corn

Add wine, broth, and onions to rice bowl at start of cooking time. Add pepper, green beans, and corn when pressure has fallen. Then replace cover but do not lock and allow rice and vegetables to steam together for 15 to 30 minutes until rice is tender.

Steamed Rice with Fruit

Substitute: Nonfat chicken broth for rice water

Add: 1/2 cup grated carrot

Add: 1/4 cup chopped onion

Add: 1/2 cup chopped dried apricots

Add: 1 tablespoon toasted sesame seeds

Add all ingredients, except sesame seeds, to rice bowl at start of cooking. Then follow steamed rice directions.

Savory Bulgur

Bulgur is precooked stone-ground wheat berries. It cooks quickly, absorbing the flavors of its cooking companions.

2 medium yellow onions, chopped
½ cup green onions, chopped
1 to 2 tablespoons chopped garlic (6 to 12 cloves)
3 cups chicken broth
2 cups bulgur
2 tablespoons pine nuts
1 teaspoon fresh thyme, or ½ teaspoon dried

Coat cooker with nonstick spray and brown onions and garlic. Add remaining ingredients, bring to high pressure quickly, and cook for 7 minutes. Reduce pressure quickly under cold water and serve.

Serves 6

Variation

Add: fresh herbs and spices such as fresh basil, fresh chili peppers, or fresh chives.

Bulgur Pilaf

For variety, leave out the canned tomatoes and add fresh mint and raw chopped Roma tomatoes along with the lemon juice and parsley after cooking. It will turn this quick salad into a Mediterranean tradition.

1 medium onion, chopped
1 tablespoon minced garlic (about 6 cloves)
1 1/2 cups chicken broth
1 cup bulgur
3 canned whole tomatoes, drained and coarsely chopped
1 teaspoon dried mint
1/2 cup minced Italian parsley
1/4 cup fresh or frozen lemon juice

Coat cooker with nonstick spray and brown onions and garlic. Add broth, bulgur, tomatoes, and mint, bring to high pressure, and cook for 10 minutes. Reduce pressure quickly under cold water, add parsley and lemon, and serve.

Serves 4

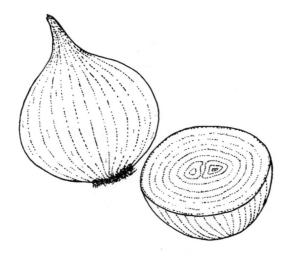

Green Pepper and Millet with Mushrooms

This mild pepper recipe is a colorful side dish and has a light, almost creamy texture that goes well with almost everything.

10 button mushrooms, cut in half
2 tablespoons fresh chopped anaheim pepper
2 tablespoons thinly sliced shallots
2 cups nonfat chicken broth
1 cup millet
3 Roma tomatoes, chopped
1 cup chopped cilantro
Salt to taste

Coat cooker with nonstick spray and brown mushrooms, pepper, and shallots. Add broth and millet, bring to high pressure, and cook for 10 minutes. Let pressure fall on its own for 10 minutes. Add tomatoes and cilantro and serve either warm or cold.

Serves 4

Vegetable Risotto

You will fall in love with this rich rice dish. Be sure to cool the cooker down quickly with water. The rice is preblanched and cooks completely through in just 5 minutes.

1 large onion, halved and thinly sliced
3 ribs celery, chopped
1 can (15-ounces) whole peeled tomatoes, drained and chopped
1 1/3 cups arborio rice
3 cups chicken broth
Grated parmesan cheese for garnish (about 1/4 cup)

Coat pan with nonstick spray. Brown onions and celery, add tomatoes and rice, and cook uncovered until rice is translucent. Pour in chicken broth, bring to high pressure quickly, and cook for 5 minutes. Cool quickly under cold water. Top with cheese and serve.

Serves 4

Barley Rice

This recipe is made with hulled barley which still contains much of its bran layer. Hulled barley is richer in flavor and nutrients than pearl barley and cooks quicker than unhulled barley. Hulled barley does not foam while cooking under pressure either.

3 1/4 cups chicken broth
1 cup short-grain brown rice
1/2 cup hulled barley
1/2 cup sliced carrots
2 tablespoons shelled pistachio nuts
1 1/2 teaspoons dried basil
2 tablespoons grated parmesan cheese

Add all ingredients, except parmesan, and cook under high pressure for 25 minutes. Let pressure fall on its own. Top with cheese and serve.

Serves 4

Variation

Add: fresh sweet pepper slices or fresh Roma tomato slices to finished dish.

Millet Pilaf

Millet is a small golden grain that is a great change of pace from rice. Whole Greek olives make a wonderful garnish for this pilaf.

1/4 cup sliced shallots
1 can (14 ounces) plum tomatoes
1 1/2 cups water or broth
1 cup millet
1 cup chopped bok choy
1 tablespoon fresh thyme

Coat cooker with nonstick spray and brown shallots. Add remaining ingredients, bring to high pressure, and cook for 10 minutes. Let pressure fall on its own.

Serves 4

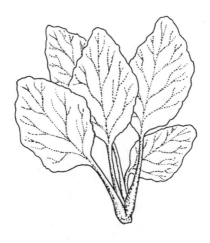

Savory Quinoa and Tomatoes

This recipe is a wonderful way to introduce yourself to quinoa. Quinoa has a delicate flavor and a light texture that almost melts in your mouth. This grain is also extremely nutritious. It contains approximately 20 percent protein and substantial amounts of iron, calcium, and phosphorus.

1 leek, chopped
1 teaspoon minced garlic
1 1/2 cups chicken broth
1 can (28 ounces) plum tomatoes, drained
1 cup quinoa

Coat pan with nonstick spray and brown leek and garlic. Add remaining ingredients, bring to high pressure quickly, and cook for 1 minute. Let pressure fall on its own for 10 minutes. Remove cover and serve.

Serves 4

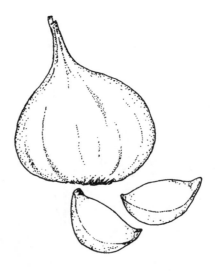

Breakfast Molasses Wheat Flakes

Sprinkle top of this breakfast grain with coconut shavings, milk and honey. We chose molasses as the sweetener because it adds a depth of flavor that plain sugar cannot match. It also contains iron, calcium, zinc, copper, and chromium which makes it a good choice for growing kids. Honey or concentrated fruit juice could also be used. Play with breakfast spices such as cinnamon, nutmeg and even a 1/2 teaspoon of vanilla extract to personalize this cereal to your liking.

2 cups water
1 cup rolled wheat flakes
1/4 cup walnuts, chopped
1 tablespoon molasses
1/4 teaspoon cardamom
Salt to taste

Coat pan with nonstick spray. Combine all ingredients, bring to high pressure quickly, and cook for only 1 minute. Remove from heat, let stand for 5 minutes, and serve.

Serves 2

Vanilla Wheat Flakes with Golden Raisins

A slice of orange peel or a few chopped dates make delightful additions, then serve with milk, honey, and fresh banana slices.

2 cups water or juice
1 cup rolled wheat flakes
1/4 cup golden raisins
1 tablespoon sliced almonds
1 teaspoon vanilla extract
1/2 teaspoon cinnamon
1/4 teaspoon nutmeg

Combine all ingredients in pressure cooker. Cook for 1 minute at high pressure then remove from heat, let stand for 5 minutes, and serve.

Serves 2

Variation

Substitute: thick rolled oats or triticale for wheat flakes.

Spicy Polenta

So quick to prepare, it can be made in a pinch. Onions, shallots, or garlic can be used in place of the leek. This is also very good reheated in a frying pan the next day.

1 leek, thinly sliced
4 cups vegetable or chicken broth
1 cup polenta
1 tablespoon chili powder
1 teaspoon paprika

Coat cooker with nonstick spray and brown leek. Add remaining ingredients, except paprika, bring to high pressure quickly, and cook for 5 minutes. Dust with the paprika and serve.

Serves 4

Coconut Rice and Shrimp

Your pressure cooker can also be used to make one-dish meals. In this recipe, the cooker is used as both a pressure cooker and a pan.

2 cups dry brown rice
1/4 cup Spanish peanuts
4 cups vegetable broth
1 tablespoon olive oil
1 pound medium raw shrimp, deveined and shelled
1/4 pound small button mushrooms
1 tablespoon chopped garlic (about 6 cloves)
1/4 cup fresh chopped basil (optional)
1/4 cup chopped mint leaves (optional)
1/4 cup chopped green onions

Sauce
1 cup unsweetened coconut milk
1/2 teaspoon Chinese chili sauce
1/2 teaspoon hot chili sesame oil
1 tablespoon cornstarch mixed with 2 tablespoons cold water
1 tablespoon lime juice

Combine all ingredients for sauce, except lime juice, in a small bowl.

Place rice, peanuts, and vegetable broth in cooker, bring to high pressure, and cook for 18 minutes. Let pressure fall on its own. Remove rice and keep warm. Coat bottom of cooker with olive oil, stir in shrimp, mushrooms, and garlic, and sauté until shrimp just turns white, about 2 minutes. Add basil, mint, and green onions, letting mixture come to a low boil. Add sauce and continue stirring until it reaches desired thickness. Stir in lime juice, then spoon sauce over rice and serve.

Serves 4

CHAPTER 13

Custards, Puddings, and Steamed Breads

*T*he pressure cooker excels at making smooth delicate custards, thick creamy puddings, rich steamed puddings, and moist steamed breads. The recipes in this chapter vary from light, low-fat delights for those watching their waistlines or hearts to rich, egg-filled treats for those occasional times we all throw caution to the wind.

Tips for Cooking Custards, Puddings, and Steamed Breads

- Steamed puddings should be cooked for the first 15 minutes without pressure, to allow the leavened batter to rise.
- Be sure to check water level after steaming and add additional water if needed for pressure-cooking. Up to a cup of water can be lost during the steaming process, leaving not enough water to bring the cooker up to pressure.
- Custards should use the quick pressure release method.

- Bread puddings and steamed puddings and breads should follow the slow release method.
- Cover top of cups with foil or wax paper to prevent condensation from falling on top of the pudding.
- To test for doneness, insert a knife into the center. If the knife comes out clean, the pudding is done. If not, continue to pressure-cook pudding for a minute or so.
- Puddings can be prepared in custard cups or any metal mold that is ovenproof and will fit into the cooker.
- Fill molds or custard cups only two thirds full to allow for expansion of the food as it cooks.
- When using aluminum foil or mold, add 1 teaspoon cream of tartar or 1 tablespoon vinegar to the water under the molds. This will prevent discoloration of the inside of the cooker.

Nutrition Tips

- When making your favorite recipe in the pressure cooker, remember it is the egg white that sets the custard. You can easily substitute an egg white for each egg yolk if cholesterol is a concern and delete the butter if calories are a concern.
- You can increase the fiber of these recipes by using whole grain breads and grains and sprinkling wheat germ on the top.
- If milk allergy or intolerance is a problem, substitute soymilk or rice milk for the milk in the recipe.
- Nuts are a great addition to many of any of these recipes, but remember that each tablespoon of nuts is loaded with fat calories. Nut oils are usually very heart healthful but they can pad your waistline.
- To make a lowfat version of any of these recipes: substitute nonfat or 1% milk for whole milk or half and half; reduce or eliminate butter and other oils; reduce or eliminate nuts and nut butters; substitute 2 egg whites for each whole egg; and reduce dry fruits and sugar.

Tapioca Pudding

A treat your children will love.

4 egg whites, slightly beaten
1/3 cup sugar
1/4 teaspoon salt
1/2 teaspoon vanilla
2 cups lowfat milk
2 tablespoons quick-cooking tapioca
1/2 cup water

Equipment
Trivet
Oiled ovenproof custard cups (4)
Cover all custard cups with a square of foil or wax paper

Add water to bottom of pressure cooker. Combine egg whites, sugar, salt, and vanilla in a bowl. Add tapioca and milk, stir, and pour into custard cups. Cover cups with wax paper or foil and place on top of trivet. Bring up to high pressure quickly and cook for 5 minutes. Reduce pressure quickly and cool in refrigerator.

Serves 4

Lemon Pudding

A wonderful, light, creamy pudding for when you want a whole-some treat to end a meal.

1/3 cup sugar
2 tablespoons flour
1/8 teaspoon salt
1 tablespoon butter
3 tablespoons fresh or frozen lemon juice
Grated rind of 1 lemon, or 2 teaspoons dried lemon zest
2 egg yolks, beaten
2/3 cup nonfat milk
2 egg whites, beaten

Equipment
Four 6-ounce custard cups
Trivet
1 cup water inside the cooker

Combine sugar, flour, salt, and butter. Add lemon juice, grated zest, egg yolks, and milk. Mix well. Fold in beaten egg whites. Coat custard cups with nonstick spray. Pour mixture into custard cups and cover securely with aluminum foil or wax paper. Place cups in prepared cooker. Bring to high pressure and cook 10 minutes and then cool quickly under cold water.

Serves 4

Variations

Orange Pudding

Substitute: 3 tablespoons concentrated orange juice for the 3 table-spoons lemon juice

Substitute: rind of ½ orange, or 1 teaspoon dried orange zest for lemon zest

Decrease: sugar to 2 tablespoons

Coconut Pudding

Substitute: coconut milk for lemon juice

Substitute: 2 tablespoons finely chopped coconut for lemon zest

Strawberry Pudding

Substitute: ¼ cup pureed fresh or frozen strawberries for 3 tablespoons lemon juice

Omit: lemon zest

Basic Egg Custard

Nothing warms up the body or soul as much as a dish of warm custard. This simple dish is extremely versatile. You can crown a dish of fruit with custard or top a dish of custard with fruit. However, like all simple dishes, the taste is directly related to the quality of the ingredients you use. Cook only with fresh eggs and milk and real vanilla. Our favorite variation is the chocolate custard.

2 cups lowfat milk
3 eggs, slightly beaten
2 tablespoons sugar
1 teaspoon vanilla
1/8 teaspoon salt
Nutmeg

Equipment
Four 6-ounce custard cups
Trivet
1 cup water inside the cooker

Coat custard cups with nonstick spray or oil. Beat together ingredients in a small bowl and fill each custard cup two thirds full. Cover securely with waxed paper or foil and place into cooker on top of trivet. Bring pressure up quickly and cook for 4 minutes. Reduce pressure quickly under cold water. Sprinkle with nutmeg and serve warm or chilled.

Variations

Rich Egg Custard

Substitute: 1 cup whole milk plus 1 cup half-and-half for 2 cups lowfat milk

Substitute: 2 whole eggs plus 2 egg yolks for 3 whole eggs

Skinny Custard

Substitute: 2 cups skim milk for lowfat milk

Substitute: 6 egg whites for 3 whole eggs

Chocolate Custard

Add: 1/2 cup premium sweetened cocoa

Omit: 2 tablespoons sugar

Caramel Custard

Prepare custard mix according to basic recipe. Press 1 1/2 table-spoons brown sugar into the bottom of each custard cup before adding custard. After cooking, when you turn the custard out of the cup onto a plate, the sugar forms a caramel sauce that cascades down the sides of the custard.

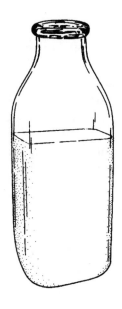

Bread and Butter Pudding

Ready to throw your stale bread out the window for the birds? Wait. By using the pressure cooker and a few staple ingredients, you can transform that bird food into an easy-to-make, warm, comforting dessert. Thickly sliced, soft-crusted French bread works well, but use any type of bread. If milk allergy is a problem, try soymilk or rice milk. Vary the type of milk, dried fruit, bread, and flavorings; any number of taste treats are possible.

8 slices of bread (stale or fresh, white, whole wheat, or mixed)
8 teaspoons butter
4 eggs, slightly beaten
2 cups lowfat milk
2 teaspoons vanilla extract
1/2 cup honey (or brown or white sugar)
1/4 cup raisins (or other dried fruit)
Ground cinnamon

Equipment
Trivet
Oiled ovenproof casserole
Cover for casserole: square of foil or wax paper

Butter each slice of bread and cut bread into 1-inch cubes. Mix eggs, milk, vanilla, and honey. Put half the bread in casserole, sprinkle half the raisins, half the milk mixture, and a dash of cinnamon. Add the rest of the bread, top with raisins, the milk, and sprinkle top with cinnamon. Cover top securely, place on trivet, and cook at high pressure for 15 minutes. Let pressure fall on its own.

Serves 4

Variations

Lowfat Bread Pudding

Substitute: 2 whole eggs plus 4 egg whites for 4 whole eggs

Substitute: nonfat evaporated milk for lowfat milk

Substitute: strawberry preserves for butter

Almond Prune Bread Pudding

Substitute: 2 teaspoons almond flavoring for 2 teaspoons vanilla

Substitute: 1/4 cup chopped pitted prunes for 1/4 cup raisins

Add: 2 tablespoons sliced almonds

Dated Bread Pudding with Caramel Sauce

Substitute: 1/4 cup chopped dates for raisins

Reduce: honey to 1/4 cup

Press 1 1/2 tablespoons brown sugar into the custard cups before adding the ingredients. After cooking, gently scrape sticking bread off the sides of the cups and unmold on plate. The brown sugar forms a caramel sauce that will puddle around the bottom of the pudding.

Onion Bread Pudding

Not a dessert, but an unusual variation on an old favorite. Serve it with dinner instead of rolls or bread.

Substitute: 2 tablespoons chopped onion plus 2 tablespoons chopped green onion for 1/4 cup raisins

Substitute: sourdough bread for French bread

Omit: honey and vanilla

Add: grated cheese sprinkled on top

Boston Brown Bread

This is our favorite brown bread recipe. The three different flours give it a unique texture. You will never go back to the canned type. This is traditionally served with beans.

1 cup yellow cornmeal
1 cup whole wheat flour
1 cup rye flour
1 teaspoon salt
4 teaspoons baking powder
1/4 teaspoon baking soda
1 3/4 cups milk
3/4 cup molasses
1 cup raisins

Equipment
Trivet, high enough to keep molds out of water
Three 1-pound oiled molds
Two cups of gently boiling water in cooker

Combine dry ingredients. Mix milk and molasses together and alternate with the raisins into flour mixture. Fill oiled molds two thirds full and cover with foil or paper. Add water and trivet to cooker and place covered molds into cooker. Remove pressure regulator from cooker and place lid on cooker. Steam 15 minutes on low heat without pressure. Replace pressure regulator and bring pressure up to 15 pounds on high heat. Cook on high pressure for an additional 30 minutes. Let pressure fall on its own. Serve bread warm or cold.

Serves 10

CHAPTER 14

Meals for One

One of the great advantages to preparing food in the pressure cooker is that a whole dinner can be cooked at the same time. The steam inside the cooker carries only heat, not flavors. Each separate vegetable, entrée, and dessert emerges from the cooker with its own particular qualities intact. And you have only one pan to clean.

There are a few simple rules for composing your meals. Obviously, all of the foods must have similar cooking times or one course will turn to mush before the other is even cooked. For example, if you want to cook a piece of meat that will need 10 minutes of cooking time, choose vegetables with a similar time such as whole potatoes, turnips, and rutabagas. But what if you want to have a steak with spinach?

If you have an entrée and want to increase the cooking time of the vegetables you can:

- use frozen vegetables
- seal vegetables in foil or a glass container

If you want to decrease cooking time:

• cut the food into smaller pieces
• cook the food directly in the cooking liquid

Another option is to quick-cool the cooker after most of the cooking is completed and then add delicate vegetables or desserts, close, and cook for the last few minutes.

Tips for Cooking for One

• Just because you are cooking for one person doesn't mean you have to buy a small pressure cooker. Remember, you can only fill the cooker two thirds full and sometimes only half full. A 6-quart cooker will only hold 3 quarts of food. If you prefer to cook in an ovenproof container inside the bowl, consider a larger model.
• To keep flavors from intermingling, cook separate courses in separate containers. Custard dishes are particularly handy. Buy them in 6-ounce and 10-ounce sizes.
• Securely cover individual courses. Water easily seeps inside.
• Do not let any part of the container rise above the two thirds mark. It can lead to blocking of the vent pipe.
• Make two or more portions of soups and stews. These foods taste even better the second day and they are easily frozen.

Nutrition Tips

• When you are composing your meals, remember that for your good health you need a minimum of five fruits and vegetables a day. Always include one fruit, a starchy vegetable, and a green or orange vegetable in your meals.
• Start the meal with a salad of leafy greens and end the meal with fruit.

Barbecue Steak with Yams and Honeyed Banana

For variety, substitute chicken for the beef, reduce total cooking time to 10 minutes, and cook the chicken along with the potato. When cooking for more than one, multiply all of the amounts except for the water.

Entrée
2 cups water
3 to 4 ounces lean round steak, trimmed of visible fat
1 yam, scrubbed and sliced
2 tablespoons barbecue sauce

Equipment
Trivet
Square of aluminum foil or wax paper

Dessert
1 unpeeled banana
1 tablespoon honey
1/8 teaspoon cinnamon

Place trivet in cooker and add water. Lay steak and yam on trivet, bring to high pressure, and cook for 20 minutes. Split banana down the middle, drizzle honey in cut, sprinkle with cinnamon, and wrap banana in paper or foil.

After 20 minutes quick-cool the cooker under cold water. Open lid, spread barbecue sauce on top of steak, and add packet with banana. Re-cover, bring again to high pressure, and cook for 10 more minutes. Cool the cooker quickly under cold water. Place steak on warmed dinner plate, adding more sauce if desired.

Stuffed Vegie Dinner with Baby Vegetables and Poached Fruit

This recipe calls for a bell pepper but use any vegetable that can be stuffed. Sweet onions are one of our favorites but zucchini, squash, and large leaf greens such as cabbage and kale will work too. We recommend simple fruit as a dessert.

Entrée
1 green pepper
1/2 cup ground chicken
1/4 cup bread crumbs
1 tablespoon chopped onion
1/8 teaspoon mixed herbs
2 tablespoons ketchup
1/4 teaspoon Worcestershire sauce
Dash salt and pepper
1/2 cup baby carrots
4 to 6 baby red potatoes

Equipment
Trivet
6-ounce custard dish
One 10 by 10-inch square wax paper or foil

Dessert
1 cooking apple (cored from top with bottom left intact)
1/8 cup chopped dates
1 tablespoon honey
Pinch cinnamon

Cut off top of pepper (or whatever vegetable you are using) and scoop out the seeds. Be careful not to perforate the wall. In a small bowl, combine chicken, bread crumbs, onion, herbs, ketchup, and Worcestershire sauce. Stuff mixture into pepper, being careful to leave room for expansion (about two thirds to three fourths full). Pour 2 cups of water into cooker and place trivet inside.

In a small bowl, combine dates, honey, and cinnamon, and stuff into apple. Coat custard cup with nonstick spray. Place apple into custard cup and wrap in a large foil or waxed paper square. Close securely.

Place stuffed pepper, baby carrots, and potatoes on top of trivet, making sure pepper does not touch sides of cooker. Lay apple packet on top of vegetables.

Bring cooker to high pressure quickly and cook for 5 minutes. Reduce pressure quickly under cold water and serve.

Variations

Stuffed Onion Dinner

Substitute: 1 large sweet onion with center scooped out (leave 2 layers of onion) for green pepper

Substitute: dried sage for mixed herbs

Substitute: 1 egg white for ketchup

Add: 1 teaspoon grated parmesan cheese sprinkled on top

Substitute: fresh orange slices and dried prunes for apple and dates

Stuffed Zucchini Dinner

Add: chopped sun-dried tomatoes

Substitute: very lean ground beef for ground chicken

Substitute: Zucchini cut in half with center scooped out for green pepper

Fill zucchini halves with beef mixture and place inside foil container or oval casserole dish. Cover securely.

Lamb Chops with Creamy Dill Sauce, Jam, and Bread Pudding

Two of our favorites. Double the recipe to share with a friend.

Entrée
2 lamb chops, trimmed of visible fat
1 medium carrot, 1/2-inch diagonal slices
4 to 5 small new potatoes
1/2 cup uncut green beans
1 cup chicken broth

Dessert
2 slices bread
1/2 cup milk
1 tablespoon strawberry preserves
1 egg, slightly beaten
2 tablespoons honey
1/2 teaspoon vanilla
1 tablespoon raisins
ground cinnamon

Sauce
1 cup yogurt
1/4 cup fresh dill

Coat bottom of cooker lightly with nonstick spray and brown meat and carrots. Add chicken broth and other entree ingredients to cooker. Place trivet on top of meat and vegetables.

Spread bread with preserves and cut bread into 8 cubes. Mix together milk, egg, honey, and vanilla. Place half of the bread into coated 10-ounce custard cup, add half of the raisins and milk mixture. Add the rest of the bread, the remaining raisins, and milk. Dust with cinnamon and securely wrap in a large square of waxed paper or foil. Place wrapped cup on top of trivet, cover, bring to high pressure and cook for 10 minutes.

While lamb is cooking, combine yogurt and fresh dill in a blender and process until smooth. Quick-cool the cooker and serve lamb with dill sauce.

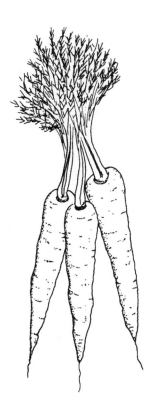

Aunt Maureen's Chicken Soup

An easy soup to make when you are sick and don't feel like cooking a big meal, guaranteed to make you feel better when you
have a cold. The garlic, mushrooms, and carrots all contain cold
and flu-fighting phytochemicals. This recipe contains enough
soup to see you through the day. Make a double batch and keep
it in the fridge. It tastes even better the next day.

$\frac{1}{2}$ pound boneless, skinless chicken thighs
1 cup chenin blanc
$\frac{1}{3}$ cup wild rice
1 $\frac{1}{2}$ teaspoons minced garlic (about 3 cloves)
1 cup shredded carrots
1 tablespoon dry vegetable broth mix
2 cups water
1 or 2 dried shiitake mushrooms, chopped into pieces

Combine all ingredients in cooker, bring to high pressure, and
cook for 20 minutes. Let pressure fall on its own.

Serves 1 or 2

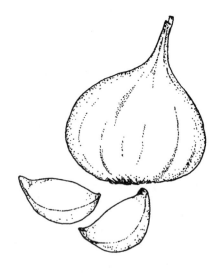

INDEX

A

Acorn squash, timetable for
cooking, 102
Advantages of pressure cooking, 8–9
Almonds
Almond Prune Bread Pudding, 169
Champagne Chicken with Shallot
Sauce and Apple Rice, 50
Nutty Wild Rice Pilaf, 147
Vanilla Wheat Flakes with Golden
Raisins, 158
Almost Instant Soup, 70–71
Anaheim peppers
Beer and Bacon Bean Soup, 80
Green Pepper and Millet with
Mushrooms, 152
Apples
Champagne Chicken with Shallot
Sauce and Apple Rice, 50
dates, 119
Mixed Fruit Compote, 122
Poached Apples, 121
Poached Fruit for one, 174–175
Pork Chops with Apples and
Roots, 27
Sweet Potato Pot Roast, 29
Apricots
Mixed Fruit Compote, 122
Steamed Rice with Fruit, 149

Artichokes
Artichokes in Garlic Sauce, 103
timetable for cooking, 99
Asparagus
Asparagus with Lemon-Dill
Sauce, 108
timetable for cooking, 99
Aunt Maureen's Chicken Soup, 178

B

Bacon and Beer Bean Soup, 80
Baked Oranges, 124
Balsamic vinegar
Hot Potato Salad, 113
Mashed Sweet Potatoes with
Balsamic Vinegar, 111
Bananas
Brown Sugar Bananas, 125
Honeyed Banana, 173
Barbecue Steak with Maple Sweet
Potatoes, 34
Barbecue Steak with Yams, 173
Barley
Chicken Soup, 74
Hearty Beef and Barley
Casserole, 35
Rice, 154
Basic Egg Custard, 166–167

Beans. *See also* specific types
  Bean and Chicken Enchiladas,
    140–141
  Bean Casserole, 132
  Beans and Greens, 132
  Beef and Bean Stew, 88–89
  Beef and Black Beans, 33
  Beer and Bacon Bean Soup, 80
  Ham and Bean Hash, 137
  Ham and Bean Soup, 71
  Hearty Multibean Soup, 77
  Mediterranean Black Beans, 133
  Minestrone, 78
  quick-soak method for, 127–128
  Refried Beans, 134
  Refried Black Beans, 131
  Savory Lentil Stew, 94
  soaking method for, 127
  Spicy Vegetable Dahl, 136
  timetable for cooking, 129–130
  White Bean Soup, 81
Beaujolais Lamb, 32
Beef
  Barbecue Steak
    with Maple Sweet
      Potatoes, 34
    with Yams, 173
  Beef and Bean Stew, 88–89
  Beef and Black Beans, 33
  Beef and Vegetable
    Casserole, 28
  Beef Borscht with Sour Cream and
    Dill, 73
  Beef Noodle Soup, 71
  Chili Pot Roast with Beans, 29
  Hearty Beef and Barley
    Casserole, 35
  Hearty Multibean Soup, 77
  Onion Soup, 79
  Quick Beef Stew, 88–89
  Stock, 68
  Stuffed Zucchini Dinner, 175
  timetable for cooking, 25
Beer
  Beer and Bacon Bean Soup, 80
  Lobster Steamed in Beer, 60
Beet greens, timetable for
  cooking, 101

Beets, 9
  Beef Borscht with Sour Cream and
    Dill, 73
  timetable for cooking, 100
Bell peppers
  Bean Casserole, 132
  Beef and Bean Stew, 89
  Chili Pot Roast with Beans, 29
  Coconut Curry Chicken, 46
  Confetti Corn, 114
  Confetti Sauce, 40
  Mediterranean Black Beans, 133
  Mild Vegetarian Chili, 139
  Pesto Zucchini and Peppers, 105
  Steamed Rice with Vegetables, 149
  Stuffed Vegie Dinner with Baby
    Vegetables, 174
  timetable for cooking, 102
  Vegetable Casserole, 104
  Vegetable Sauces, 58
  White Bean Soup, 81
Black beans
  Bean and Chicken Enchiladas,
    140–141
  Beef and Black Beans, 33
  Refried Black Beans, 131
Black Forest Ham, French Navy Bean
  Soup, 82
Blockages in vent tube, 6
Blueberries in Raisin Topping, 123
Blue cheese in Vinaigrette Sauces, 58
Boiling points, 7–8
Bok choy
  Beans and Greens, 132
  Millet Pilaf, 155
Borscht with Sour Cream and Dill, 73
Boston Brown Bread, 170
Bread and Butter Pudding, 168–169
Breads. *See* Steamed breads
Breakfast Molasses Wheat Flakes, 157
Broccoli
  timetable for cooking, 100
  Vegetable Casserole, 104
Browning, 10–11, 16
Brown rice
  Barley Rice, 154
  Coconut Rice and Shrimp, 160
  Moroccan Bean and Rice Stew, 92

Rice Pilaf, 146
Steamed Rice, 148
Brown Sugar Bananas, 125
Brussels sprouts, timetable for
     cooking, 100
Bulgur
  Hearty Multibean Soup, 77
  Pilaf, 151
  Savory Bulgur, 150
Burning on bottom, 17, 19
Butternut squash in Saffron Seafood
     Stew, 96

C

Cabbage
  Beef Borscht with Sour Cream and
       Dill, 73
  timetable for cooking, 100
Cannellini beans
  Bean Casserole, 132
  Beer and Bacon Bean Soup, 80
  Cannellini Bean and Swiss Chard
       Soup, 83
  Hearty Multibean Soup, 77
  Spicy Vegetable Bean Stew, 91
  White Bean Soup, 81
Capers
  Vinaigrette Sauces, 58
  Yogurt Sauces, 57
Caramel Custard, 167
Carrots
  Almost Instant Soup, 70–71
  Aunt Maureen's Chicken Soup, 178
  Barley Rice, 154
  Beef and Black Beans, 33
  Beef and Vegetable Casserole, 28
  Beef Borscht with Sour Cream and
       Dill, 73
  Cannellini Beans and Swiss Chard
       Soup, 83
  Chicken Soup, 74
  Creamed Turkey Casserole, 45
  French Navy Bean Soup, 82
  Glazed Carrots and Shallots, 109
  Hearty Beef and Barley
       Casserole, 35
  Lamb Stew, 87

Minestrone, 78
Pesto Zucchini and Peppers, 105
Poached Fish with Julienned
     Vegetables, 56
Pork Chops with Apples and
     Roots, 27
Pot Roast with Onions and Root
     Vegetables, 31
Poultry Casserole, 44
Quick and Easy White Rice
     Pilaf, 146
Quick Beef Stew, 88–89
Savory Lentil Stew, 94
Seafood and Saffron Soup, 76
Spicy Vegetable Bean Stew, 91
Steamed Rice with Fruit, 149
Stuffed Vegie Dinner with Baby
     Vegetables, 174
timetable for cooking, 100
Vegetable Casserole, 104
White Bean Soup, 81
Cashews in Hot Nutty Game
     Hens, 51
Casseroles
  Bean Casserole, 132
  Beef and Vegetable Casserole, 28
  Creamed Turkey Casserole, 45
  Frozen Vegie Casserole, 105
  Hearty Beef and Barley
       Casserole, 35
  Pesto Zucchini and Peppers, 105
  Vegetable Casserole, 104
Cauliflower
  timetable for cooking, 100
  Vegetable Casserole, 104
Celery
  Beef Borscht with Sour Cream and
       Dill, 73
  Beer and Bacon Bean Soup, 80
  Cannellini Beans and Swiss Chard
       Soup, 83
  Chicken Soup, 74
  French Navy Bean Soup, 82
  Mild Vegetarian Chili, 139
  Minestrone, 78
  Quick Beef Stew, 88–89
  Savory Lentil Stew, 94
  timetable for cooking, 100

Celery, continued
  Vegetable Risotto, 153
  Vegetable Sauces, 58
  White Bean Soup, 81
Champagne Chicken with Shallot
      Sauce and Apple Rice, 50
Cheddar cheese in Bean and Chicken
      Enchiladas, 140–141
Cheese. *See also* specific types
  Cheese Sauce, 107
Cherries in Raisin Topping, 123
Chicken
  Almost Instant Soup, 70–71
  Aunt Maureen's Chicken
        Soup, 178
  Bean and Chicken Enchiladas,
        140–141
  Champagne Chicken with Shallot
        Sauce and Apple Rice, 50
  Chicken Garlic Soup with
        Greens, 70
  Chicken Soup, 74
  Chick-peas and Chicken, 138
  and Chick-pea Stew, 90
  Chunky Chicken Soup, 71
  Coconut Curry Chicken, 46
  Confetti Sauce, 40
  and Dumpling Casserole, 48
  Ginger Chicken, 44–45
  Hawaiian Chicken, 47
  nutrition tips, 38
  Poached Chicken, 40–41
  Poultry Casserole, 44
  sauces for, 40–41
  Savory Lentil Stew, 94
  Sherry Chicken with Garlic, 42
  Sour Cream and Dill Sauce, 41
  Stew, 89
  Stock, 68–69
  Stuffed Vegie Dinner with Baby
        Vegetables, 174
  timetable for cooking, 39
  tips for cooking, 37–38
  Warm Curry Sauce, 41
Chick-peas
  Chicken and Chick-pea Stew, 90
  Chick-peas and Chicken, 138
  Hearty Multibean Soup, 77

Moroccan Bean and Rice Stew, 92
  Spicy Vegetable Bean Stew, 91
Chiles
  Cocktail Sauce, Chipotle, 56
  Hearty Multibean Soup, 77
  Spicy Beans, 132
  Spicy Vegetable Bean Stew, 91
  Vegetable Sauces, 58
  White Bean Soup, 81
  Yogurt Sauces, 57
Chili, Mild Vegetarian, 139
Chili Pot Roast with Beans, 29
Chipotle Cocktail Sauce, 56
Chocolate
  Chocolate Custard, 167
  Poached Company Fruit, 120–121
Chunky Chicken Soup, 71
Cilantro
  Bean and Chicken Enchiladas,
        140–141
  Beef and Black Beans, 33
  Green Pepper and Millet with
        Mushrooms, 152
  Moroccan Bean and Rice Stew, 92
Cioppino, 93
Clams
  Cioppino, 93
  New England Clam Chowder, 75
  Steamed Clams, 61
Cleaning stains on cooker, 6, 19
Clogged vent tube, 18
Coconut
  Coconut Pudding, 165
  Coconut Rice and Shrimp, 160
  Curry Chicken, Coconut, 46
  Fish and Eggplant Curry, 64
  Whole Fish in Red Curry Sauce
        with Lime Leaves, 63
Cod
  Saffron Seafood Stew, 96
  Seafood and Saffron Soup, 76
Collards
  Chicken Garlic Soup with
        Greens, 70
  timetable for cooking, 100
Common problems, 17–18
Compote, Mixed Fruit, 122–123
Confetti Corn, 114

Confetti Sauce, 40
Cooking times, 9–10
Corn
    Confetti Corn, 114
    Frozen Vegie Casserole, 105
    Ham and Bean Hash, 137
    New England Clam
        Chowder, 75
    Steamed Rice with Vegetables, 149
    timetable for cooking, 100
    Vegetable Sauces, 58
Crab Sauce, Hot, 106
Cranberries
    Nutty Wild Rice Pilaf, 147
    Raisin Topping, 123
Creamed Turkey Casserole, 45
Creamy Dill Sauce, 106
Cucumber in Vegetable Sauces, 58
Custards. *See also* Puddings
    Basic Egg Custard, 166–167
    Caramel Custard, 167
    Chocolate Custard, 167
    nutrition tips, 162
    Rich Egg Custard, 166
    Skinny Custard, 167
    tips for cooking, 161–162

D

Dahl, Spicy Vegetable, 136
Dates
    Dated Bread Pudding with Caramel
        Sauce, 169
    Date-stuffed Apples, 119
    Pineapple Pork with Honey Date
        Yams and Pearl Onion
        Peas, 30
    Poached Fruit for one, 174–175
Dill
    Beef Borscht with Sour Cream and
        Dill, 73
    Creamy Dill Sauce, 106
    Lamb Chops with Creamy Dill
        Sauce, 176–177
    Lemon-Dill Sauce, 108
    Sour Cream and Dill Sauce, 41
Discolorations of cooker, 19–20
Do's and don'ts, 13–14

Dried fruits
    Mixed Fruit Compote, 122–123
    Stewed Dried Fruit, 121
    timetables for cooking, 117–118
Duck, nutrition tips for, 38

E

Eggplant
    Chicken and Chick-pea Stew, 90
    Fish and Eggplant Curry, 64
    timetable for cooking, 101
Eggs. *See also* Custards
    Hot Potato Salad, 113
Enchiladas, Bean and Chicken,
    140–141
European Pea Soup, 72

F

Fennel
    Spicy Vegetable Dahl, 136
    Vegetable Sauces, 58
Feta cheese
    Tomatoes and Beans, 132
    Vinaigrette Sauces, 58
Fish. *See* Seafood
Fish and Eggplant Curry, 64
4-quart models, 3–4
French Navy Bean Soup, 82
Frozen Vegie Casserole, 105
Fruits. *See also* Dried fruits; specific
        types
    dried fruit, tips for cooking, 116
    fresh fruits, timetables for cooking,
        117–118
    Mixed Fruit Compote, 122–123
    Poached Company
        Fruit, 120–121
    Steamed Rice with Fruit, 149
    timetables for cooking, 117–118
    tips for cooking, 115–116
Fruit Sauces, 58

G

Game, timetable for cooking, 25
Garbanzo beans. *See* Chick-peas

Garlic
  Artichokes in Garlic Sauce, 103
  Aunt Maureen's Chicken Soup, 178
  Beef and Black Beans, 33
  browning garlic, 10–11
  Bulgur Pilaf, 151
  Chicken and Chick-pea Stew, 90
  Chicken Garlic Soup with
      Greens, 70
  Chick-peas and Chicken, 138
  Cioppino, 93
  Coconut Curry Chicken, 46
  Coconut Rice and Shrimp, 160
  Hawaiian Chicken, 47
  Hot Nutty Game Hens, 51
  Lentil Hummus, 135
  Mediterranean Black Beans, 133
  Minestrone, 78
  Refried Beans, 134
  Refried Black Beans, 131
  Saffron Seafood Stew, 96
  Savory Bulgur, 150
  Savory Quinoa and Tomatoes, 156
  Seafood and Saffron Soup, 76
  Sherry Chicken with Garlic, 42
  Spicy Vegetable Bean Stew, 91
  Vinaigrette Sauces, 58
  White Bean Soup, 81
  Yogurt Sauces, 57
Gasket, 3, 4
  replacement of, 18–19
Ginger
  Coconut Curry Chicken, 46
  Ginger Chicken, 44–45
  Ginger-Tomato Spaghetti Sauce, 110
  Hawaiian Chicken, 47
  Hot Nutty Game Hens, 51
  Mixed Fruit Compote, 122
  Spicy Ginger Compote, 122
  Spicy Vegetable Dahl, 136
  Yogurt Sauces, 57
Glazed Carrots and Shallots, 109
Gouda cheese in Bean and Chicken
      Enchiladas, 140–141
Grains, 4. See also specific types
  nutrition tips, 144
  timetables for steaming, 145
  tips for cooking, 143–144

Grapefruit
  Baked Grapefruit, 124
  Fruit Sauces, 58
Green beans
  Frozen Vegie Casserole, 105
  Minestrone, 78
  Poached Fish with Julienned
      Vegetables, 56
  Steamed Rice with Vegetables, 149
  timetable for cooking, 99
  with Tomatoes and Sesame
      Seeds, 112
Green bell peppers. See Bell peppers
Green onions
  Coconut Rice and Shrimp, 160
  Confetti Sauce, 40
  Creamy Dill Sauce, 106
  Fruit Sauces, 58
  Hot Potato Salad, 113
  Orange Roughy with Mango, 62
  Savory Bulgur, 150
  Steamed Rice with Vegetables, 149
Green Pepper and Millet with Mush-
      rooms, 152

H

Ham
  European Pea Soup, 72
  French Navy Bean Soup, 82
  Ham and Bean Hash, 137
  Ham and Bean Soup, 71
  New England Clam Chowder, 75
  timetable for cooking, 25
Hawaiian Chicken, 47
Hearty Beef and Barley
      Casserole, 35
Hearty Multibean Soup, 77
High-pressure weight, 4
Hints for pressure cooking, 12–13
Honeyed Banana, 173
Hot Crab Sauce, 106
Hot Curry Sauce, 107
Hot Nutty Game Hens, 51
Hot Potato Salad, 113
Hubbard squash, timetable for
      cooking, 102
Hummus, Lentil, 135

I

India, use in, 21–22
Italian Turkey Legs, 43

J

Jam and Bread Pudding, 176–177
Japan, use in, 21

K

Kale
    Beef and Black Beans, 33
    Chicken Garlic Soup with Greens, 70
    timetable for cooking, 100–101
Kidney beans
    Beef and Bean Stew, 89
    Chili Pot Roast with Beans, 29
    Ham and Bean Hash, 137
    Ham and Bean Soup, 71
    Mexican-Style Turkey, 43
    Mild Vegetarian Chili, 139
    Spicy Beans, 132
Kiwis, Fruit Sauces for, 58
Kohlrabi
    Hearty Beef and Barley
        Casserole, 35
    timetable for cooking, 101

L

Lamb
    Beaujolais Lamb, 32
    Lamb Chops with Creamy Dill
        Sauce, 176–177
    Stew, 87
    timetable for cooking, 25
Leeks
    Almost Instant Soup, 70–71
    Bean Casserole, 132
    Beef and Black Beans, 33
    browning leeks, 10–11
    Chicken Stew, 89
    Hearty Beef and Barley Casserole, 35
    Savory Quinoa and Tomatoes, 156
    Spicy Polenta, 159
    Sweet Potato Pot Roast, 29
Legumes. *See* Beans

Lemons
    Lemon-Dill Sauce, 108
    Lemon Pudding, 164
    Lemon-Tarragon Vinaigrette, 57
    Mayonnaise Sauces, 57–58
Lentils
    Hearty Multibean Soup, 77
    Lentil Hummus, 135
    Moroccan Bean and Rice Stew, 92
    Potato, Lentil, and Wild Mush-
        room Stew, 95
    Savory Lentil Stew, 94
Lid shapes, 3
Lift pin, 3, 5
    blockages in, 6
Lima beans
    Frozen Vegie Casserole, 105
    timetable for cooking, 100
Lime
    Mayonnaise Sauces, 57–58
    Orange Roughy with Mango, 62
Lime leaves
    Seafood and Saffron Soup, 76
    Whole Fish in Red Curry Sauce
        with Lime Leaves, 63
Liquids, 4
    suitability of, 16
Lobster Steamed in Beer, 60
Lowfat Bread Pudding, 169

M

Maintenance of cooker, 6, 19–20
Mangoes
    Fruit Sauces, 58
    Orange Roughy with Mango, 62
Mashed Sweet Potatoes with
        Balsamic Vinegar, 111
Mayonnaise
    Sauces, 57–58
    Warm Curry Sauce, 41
Meals for one, 171–178
Meats, 9. *See also* specific meats
    browning meat, 10–11
    nutrition tips for, 24
    questions about, 16
    timetable for cooking, 25–26
    tips for cooking, 23–24

Mediterranean Black Beans, 133
Mediterranean recipes, 22
Mexican-Style Turkey, 43
Mild Vegetarian Chili, 139
Millet
    Green Pepper and Millet with
        Mushrooms, 152
    Millet Pilaf, 155
Minestrone, 78
Mixed Fruit Compote, 122–123
Molasses
    Boston Brown Bread, 170
    Breakfast Molasses Wheat Flakes, 157
    Savory Lentil Stew, 94
Moroccan Bean and Rice Stew, 92
Mushroom Pilaf, 147
Mushrooms
    Aunt Maureen's Chicken Soup, 178
    browning mushrooms, 10–11
    Chicken Stew, 89
    Coconut Rice and Shrimp, 160
    Green Pepper and Millet with
        Mushrooms, 152
Potato, Lentil, and Wild Mushroom
    Stew, 95

                           N

Navy beans
    French Navy Bean Soup, 82
    Minestrone, 78
    White Bean Soup, 81
New England Clam Chowder, 75
Nutty Wild Rice Pilaf, 147

                           O

Odors, 9
Olives in Tomatoes and Beans, 132
One, meals for, 171–178
Onions. See also Green onions
    Almost Instant Soup, 70–71
    Bean Casserole, 132
    Beaujolais Lamb, 32
    Beef and Vegetable Casserole, 28
    Beef Borscht with Sour Cream and
        Dill, 73
    browning onions, 10–11

Bulgur Pilaf, 151
Cannellini Beans and Swiss Chard
    Soup, 83
Chicken and Chick-pea
    Stew, 90
Chick-peas and Chicken, 138
Coconut Curry Chicken, 46
Confetti Corn, 114
French Navy Bean Soup, 82
Green Beans with Tomatoes and
    Sesame Seeds, 112
Ham and Bean Hash, 137
Hearty Beef and Barley
    Casserole, 35
Hearty Multibean Soup, 77
Hot Nutty Game Hens, 51
Lamb Stew, 87
Lentil Hummus, 135
Mediterranean Black Beans, 133
Minestrone, 78
Moroccan Bean and
    Rice Stew, 92
Onion Bread Pudding, 169
Onion Soup, 79
Pineapple Pork with Honey Date
    Yams and Pearl Onion
    Peas, 30
Pork Chops with Apples and
    Roots, 27
Pot Roast with Onions and Root
    Vegetables, 31
Quick and Easy White Rice
    Pilaf, 146
Refried Beans, 134
Refried Black Beans, 131
Saffron Seafood Stew, 96
Savory Bulgur, 150
Savory Lentil Stew, 94
Seafood and Saffron Soup, 76
Spicy Vegetable Bean Stew, 91
Spicy Vegetable Dahl, 136
Steamed Rice with Fruit, 149
Stuffed Onion Dinner, 175
timetable for cooking, 101
Vegetable Casserole, 104
Vegetable Risotto, 153
Yogurt Sauces, 57
Orange Roughy with Mango, 62

Oranges
Baked Oranges, 124
Orange Pudding, 164–165
Overheating cooker, 20
Overpressure plug, 3, 5
replacement of, 18–19

P

Papaya, Fruit Sauces for, 58
Parsnips, timetable for cooking, 101
Parts of cooker, 3–6
Pasta
Beef Noodle Soup, 71
Minestrone, 78
Peanuts in Coconut Rice and
Shrimp, 160
Pears
Mixed Fruit Compote, 122
Poached Company Fruit, 120–121
Peas
Chunky Chicken Soup, 71
Confetti Corn, 114
Pineapple Pork with Honey Date
Yams and Pearl Onion
Peas, 30
Quick and Easy White Rice
Pilaf, 146
timetable for cooking, 101
Vegetable Casserole, 104
Pesto Zucchini and Peppers, 105
Pilafs
Bulgur Pilaf, 151
Millet Pilaf, 155
Nutty Wild Rice Pilaf, 147
Rice Pilaf, 146
Pineapple
Fruit Sauces, 58
Hawaiian Chicken, 47
Pork with Honey Date Yams and
Pearl Onion Peas, 30
Pine nuts in Savory Bulgur, 150
Pinto beans
Mild Vegetarian Chili, 139
Refried Beans, 134
Pistachio nuts in Barley Rice, 154
Plums, Fruit Sauces for, 58
Poached Chicken, 40–41

Poached Company Fruit, 120–121
Poached Fish with Julienned Vege-
tables, 56
Poached Fruit for one, 174–175
Polenta, Spicy, 159
Pork. See also Ham
Pineapple Pork with Honey Date
Yams and Pearl Onion
Peas, 30
Pork Chops with Apples and
Roots, 27
timetable for cooking, 25
Potatoes, 9
Beef and Vegetable Casserole, 28
Beef Borscht with Sour Cream and
Dill, 73
Cannellini Beans and Swiss Chard
Soup, 83
Chicken Soup, 74
Chunky Chicken Soup, 71
Creamed Turkey Casserole, 45
Ham and Bean Hash, 137
Hearty Beef and Barley
Casserole, 35
Hot Potato Salad, 113
Lamb Stew, 87
Minestrone, 78
New England Clam Chowder, 75
Pork Chops with Apples and
Roots, 27
Potato, Lentil, and Wild Mush-
room Stew, 95
Pot Roast with Onions and Root
Vegetables, 31
Poultry Casserole, 44
Quick Beef Stew, 88–89
Saffron Seafood Stew, 96
Sherry Chicken with Garlic, 42
Stuffed Vegie Dinner with Baby
Vegetables, 174
timetable for cooking, 101
Turkey-Vegetable Stew, 89
Two Can Turkey, 43
Pot Roast
Beef and Vegetable
Casserole, 28
with Onions and Root
Vegetables, 31

Poultry, 37–40. *See also* Chicken;
    Turkey
  Hot Nutty Game Hens, 51
  Poultry Casserole, 44
  timetable for cooking, 39
  tips for cooking, 37–38
Pressure cooking, 11
Pressure pop-up valve, 3, 5
Pressure regulator, 4
Pressure steaming, 10
Prunes
  Almond Prune Bread
    Pudding, 169
  Mixed Fruit Compote, 122
Puddings. *See also* Custards
  Almond Prune Bread
    Pudding, 169
  Bread and Butter Pudding, 168–169
  Coconut Pudding, 165
  Dated Bread Pudding with Caramel
    Sauce, 169
  Jam and Bread Pudding, 176–177
  Lemon Pudding, 164
  Lowfat Bread Pudding, 169
  nutrition tips, 162
  Onion Bread Pudding, 169
  Orange Pudding, 164–165
  Strawberry Pudding, 165
  Tapioca Pudding, 163
  tips for cooking, 161–162
Pumpkin, timetable for cooking, 101

Q

Quick and Easy White Rice
  Pilaf, 146
Quick Beef Stew, 88–89
Quick release under water, 12
Quick steam release button, 12
Quinoa, Savory, and Tomatoes, 156

R

Raisins
  Barbecue Steak with Maple Sweet
    Potatoes, 34
  Raisin Topping for Mixed Fruit
    Compote, 123

Vanilla Wheat Flakes with Golden
    Raisins, 158
Red bell peppers. *See* Bell peppers
Refried Beans, 134
Refried Black Beans, 131
Releasing pressure, 11–12
Rice. *See also* Brown rice
  Champagne Chicken with Shallot
    Sauce and Apple Rice, 50
  Rice Pilaf, 146
  Steamed Rice, 148
  Steamed Seasoned White Rice, 148
  Vegetable Risotto, 153
Rich Egg Custard, 166
Risotto, Vegetable, 153
Ristra, 91
Rock or hiss of cooker, 16
Rutabagas, 9
  Pork Chops with Apples and
    Roots, 27
  timetable for cooking, 101

S

Safety release lock, 5
Saffron
  Moroccan Bean and Rice Stew, 92
  Saffron Seafood Stew, 96
  Seafood and Saffron Soup, 76
Salad, Hot Potato, 113
Salmon Sauce, 106
Sauces
  Cheese Sauce, 107
  Chipotle Cocktail Sauce, 56
  Coconut Curry Chicken, sauce
    for, 46
  Confetti Sauce, 40
  Creamy Dill Sauce, 106
  Fruit Sauces, 58
  Ginger-Tomato Spaghetti Sauce, 110
  Hot Crab Sauce, 106
  Hot Curry Sauce, 107
  Lemon-Dill Sauce, 108
  Lemon-Tarragon Vinaigrette, 57
  Mayonnaise Sauces, 57–58
  Salmon Sauce, 106
  for seafood, 56–58
  Shallot Sauce, 50

Sour Cream and Dill Sauce, 41
  for vegetables, 106–107
  Vegetable Sauces, 58
  Vinaigrette Sauces, 58
  Warm Curry Sauce, 41
  Yogurt Sauces, 57
Sausage in Potato, Lentil, and Wild
      Mushroom Stew, 95
Savory Bulgur, 150
Savory Lentil Stew, 94
Savory Quinoa and Tomatoes, 156
Scallops in Seafood and Saffron
      Soup, 76
Seafood, 53. *See also* specific types
  buying seafood, tips for, 54–55
  Chipotle Cocktail Sauce, 56
  Cioppino, 93
  Fish and Eggplant Curry, 64
  Fruit Sauces, 58
  Hot Crab Sauce, 106
  Lemon-Tarragon Vinaigrette, 57
  Lobster Steamed in Beer, 60
  Mayonnaise Sauces, 57–58
  nutrition tips for, 54
  Orange Roughy with Mango, 62
  Poached Fish with Julienned
        Vegetables, 56
  Saffron Seafood Stew, 96
  Salmon Sauce, 106
  Seafood and Saffron Soup, 76
  Shrimp in Spicy Marinade, 59
  Steamed Clams, 61
  timetable for cooking, 55
  tips for cooking, 53–55
  Vinaigrette Sauces, 58
  Whole Fish in Red Curry Sauce
        with Lime Leaves, 63
  Yogurt Sauces, 57
Sea level boiling point, 7–8
Sealing ring, 3, 4
  replacement of, 18–19
Sesame seeds
  Green Beans with Tomatoes and
        Sesame Seeds, 112
  Steamed Rice with Fruit, 149
Shallots
  Champagne Chicken with Shallot
        Sauce and Apple Rice, 50

Ginger-Tomato Spaghetti Sauce, 110
Glazed Carrots and Shallots, 109
Green Pepper and Millet with
      Mushrooms, 152
Millet Pilaf, 155
Sherry
  Ginger Chicken, 44–45
  Hawaiian Chicken, 47
  Sherry Chicken with Garlic, 42
Shrimp
  Coconut Rice and Shrimp, 160
  Seafood and Saffron Soup, 76
  Shrimp in Spicy Marinade, 59
6–8 quart models, 4
Skinny Custard, 167
Slow-release method, 11
Soups
  Almost Instant Soup, 70–71
  Aunt Maureen's Chicken Soup, 178
  Beef Borscht with Sour Cream and
        Dill, 73
  Beef Noodle Soup, 71
  Beef Stock, 68
  Beer and Bacon Bean Soup, 80
  Cannellini Beans and Swiss Chard
        Soup, 83
  Chicken Soup, 74
  Chicken Stock, 68–69
  Chunky Chicken Soup, 71
  European Pea Soup, 72
  French Navy Bean Soup, 82
  Ham and Bean Soup, 71
  Hearty Multibean Soup, 77
  Minestrone, 78
  New England Clam Chowder, 75
  nutrition tips, 66
  Seafood and Saffron Soup, 76
  stocks, 67–68
  timetable for cooking, 67
  tips for cooking, 65–66
  Vegetable Broth, 69
  White Bean Soup, 81
Sour cream
  Beef Borscht with Sour Cream and
        Dill, 73
  Confetti Sauce, 40
  Hot Potato Salad, 113
  Sour Cream and Dill Sauce, 41

Spain, use in, 21
Spicy Beans, 132
Spicy Ginger Compote, 122
Spicy Polenta, 159
Spicy Vegetable Bean Stew, 91
Spicy Vegetable Dahl, 136
Spinach in Chicken Garlic Soup with
     Greens, 70
Split peas
    European Pea Soup, 72
    Spicy Vegetable Dahl, 136
Squash. See also specific types
    Saffron Seafood Stew, 96
    timetable for cooking, 102
Stains on cooker, 6
Steamed breads
    Boston Brown Bread, 170
    nutrition tips, 162
    tips for cooking, 161–162
Steamed Clams, 61
Steamed Rice, 148
Steamed Rice with Fruit, 149
Steamed Rice with Vegetables, 149
Steamed Seasoned White
     Rice, 148
Steamer basket, 5–6, 10
Steaming grains. See Grains
Stewed Dried Fruit, 121
Stews
    Beef and Bean Stew, 88–89
    Chicken and Chick-pea Stew, 90
    Chicken Stew, 89
    Cioppino, 93
    Lamb Stew, 87
    Moroccan Bean and Rice
        Stew, 92
    nutrition tips for, 86
    Potato, Lentil, and Wild Mush-
        room Stew, 95
    Quick Beef Stew, 88–89
    Saffron Seafood Stew, 96
    Savory Lentil Stew, 94
    Spicy Vegetable Bean Stew, 91
    tips for cooking, 85–86
    Turkey-Vegetable Stew, 89
Sticking food, 17
Stocks, 67–68
    Beef Stock, 68

Chicken Stock, 68–69
    Vegetable Broth, 69
Strawberries
    Fruit Sauces, 58
    Strawberry Pudding, 165
Stuffed Onion Dinner, 175
Stuffed Vegie Dinner with Baby
     Vegetables, 174
Stuffed Zucchini Dinner, 175
Sultanas in Raisin Topping, 123
Sweet peppers. See Bell peppers
Sweet potatoes, 9
    Barbecue Steak with Maple Sweet
        Potatoes, 34
    Ginger Chicken, 44–45
    Mashed Sweet Potatoes with
        Balsamic Vinegar, 111
    Pork Chops with Apples and
        Roots, 27
    Pot Roast, Sweet Potato, 29
    Pot Roast with Onions and Root
        Vegetables, 31
    timetable for cooking, 101
    Turkey-Vegetable Stew, 89
Swiss chard
    Cannellini Beans and Swiss Chard
        Soup, 83
    Spicy Vegetable Bean Stew, 91
    timetable for cooking, 101

T

Tapioca Pudding, 163
Time-savers, cookers as, 15
Timetables
    beans, timetable for, 129–130
    dried fruits, timetables for cooking,
        117–118
    fresh fruits, timetables for
        cooking, 117
    fresh vegetable timetables,
        99–102
    frozen vegetable timetables, 99
    fruits, timetables for cooking,
        117–118
    grains, timetables for steaming, 145
    poultry timetables, 39
    red meat timetables, 25–26

seafood timetable, 55
soup timetables, 67
vegetable timetables, 99–102
Tomatoes
    Beef and Bean Stew, 88–89
    Beef and Black Beans, 33
    Beef Borscht with Sour Cream and
        Dill, 73
    Beer and Bacon Bean Soup, 80
    Bulgur Pilaf, 151
    Chicken and Chick-pea Stew, 90
    Chunky Chicken Soup, 71
    Cioppino, 93
    Ginger-Tomato Spaghetti
        Sauce, 110
    Green Beans with Tomatoes and
        Sesame Seeds, 112
    Green Pepper and Millet with
        Mushrooms, 152
    Ham and Bean Hash, 137
    Mediterranean Black Beans, 133
    Mild Vegetarian Chili, 139
    Millet Pilaf, 155
    Minestrone, 78
    Moroccan Bean and Rice
        Stew, 92
    Mushroom Pilaf, 147
    Pesto Zucchini and Peppers, 105
    Pot Roast, Tomato, 28
    Saffron Seafood Stew, 96
    Savory Quinoa and Tomatoes, 156
    Sherry Chicken with Garlic, 42
    Spicy Vegetable Dahl, 136
    timetable for cooking, 102
    Tomatoes and Beans, 132
    Tomato Turkey Breast with
        Rosemary and Oregano, 49
    Two Can Turkey, 43
    Vegetable Risotto, 153
    Yogurt Sauces, 57
Topping, Raisin, 123
Trivet, 5–6, 10
Troubleshooting, 18–19
Turkey
    Bean and Turkey Enchiladas, 140–141
    Creamed Turkey Casserole, 45
    Italian Turkey Legs, 43
    Mexican-Style Turkey, 43

    nutrition tips, 38
    timetable for cooking, 39
    tips for cooking, 37–38
    Tomato Turkey Breast with
        Rosemary and Oregano, 49
    Turkey-Vegetable Stew, 89
    Two Can Turkey, 43
Turnip greens, timetable for
    cooking, 101
Turnips, 9
    Pot Roast with Onions and Root
        Vegetables, 31
    Spicy Vegetable Bean Stew, 91
    timetable for cooking, 101
Two Can Turkey, 43

V

Vanilla Wheat Flakes with Golden
    Raisins, 158
Veal, timetable for cooking, 25
Vegetable Broth, 69
Vegetables. See also specific types
    Cheese Sauce, 107
    Creamy Dill Sauce, 106
    fresh vegetables, timetable for
        cooking, 99–100
    frozen vegetables, timetable for
        cooking, 99
    Frozen Vegie Casserole, 105
    Hot Crab Sauce, 106
    Hot Curry Sauce, 107
    nutrition tips for, 98
    Risotto, 153
    Salmon Sauce, 106
    sauces for, 106–107
    Steamed Rice with Vege-
        tables, 149
    Stuffed Vegie Dinner with Baby
        Vegetables, 174
    timetables for cooking, 99–102
    tips for cooking, 97–98
    Vegetable Casserole, 104
    Vegetable Sauces, 58
Vent tube, 4
    clogged vent tube, 18
Versatility of cooker, 9
Vinaigrette Sauces, 58

W

Walnuts in Breakfast Molasses Wheat
    Flakes, 157
Warm Curry Sauce, 41
Washing the cooker, 6
Water, quick release under, 12
Watery recipes, 17–18
Weight, 4
Weight, purpose of, 9
Wheat flakes
    Breakfast Molasses Wheat
        Flakes, 157
    Vanilla Wheat Flakes with Golden
        Raisins, 158
White Bean Soup, 81
Whole Fish in Red Curry Sauce with
    Lime Leaves, 63
Wild rice
    Aunt Maureen's Chicken Soup, 178
    Nutty Wild Rice Pilaf, 147

Y

Yams, 9
    Barbecue Steak with Maple Sweet
        Potatoes, 34

Barbecue Steak with Yams, 173
Pineapple Pork with Honey Date
        Yams and Pearl Onion
        Peas, 30
timetable for cooking, 101
Yogurt
    Cheese Sauce, 107
    Confetti Sauce, 40
    Creamed Turkey Casserole, 45
    Hot Curry Sauce, 107
    Hot Nutty Game Hens, 51
    Sauces, 57
    Shallot Sauce, 50
    Warm Curry Sauce, 41

Z

Zucchini
    Creamed Turkey Casserole, 45
    Minestrone, 78
    Pesto Zucchini and Peppers, 105
    Poached Fish with Julienned
        Vegetables, 56
    Stuffed Zucchini Dinner, 175
    timetable for cooking, 102
    Vegetable Casserole, 104